HOW TO USE THE
FREEDOM OF INFORMATION ACT (FOIA)

HOW TO USE THE
FREEDOM OF INFORMATION ACT (FOIA)

L. G. SHERICK

ARCO PUBLISHING COMPANY, INC.
NEW YORK

To My Parents
(One and All)

Published by Arco Publishing Company, Inc.
219 Park Avenue South, New York, N.Y. 10003

Copyright © 1978 by L.G. Sherick

Library of Congress Cataloging in Publication Data

Sherick, L G
  How to use the Freedom of information act (FOIA)
  Includes index.
  1. Government information—United States.
2. Public records—Law and legislation—United States.
I. Title.
KF5753.S53   342'.73'085   78-7353
ISBN 0-688-04643-0
ISBN 0-688-04651-1 pbk.

Printed in the United States of America

Contents

Introduction

"The right to receive information and ideas is fundamental for our free society."—SUPREME COURT OF THE UNITED STATES

As we Americans have painfully learned, secrecy in our government creates an environment for a Watergate, a Vietnam and a Bay of Pigs. For too long high elected officials have disregarded the wise advice of President Abraham Lincoln to the effect that "Let the people know the facts and the country will be saved."

There are fundamental things which separate our representative system of government from a dictatorship, according to the Honorable John E. Moss, Representative from California. They include:

1. free elections;
2. freedom of information; and
3. faith in the good sense of the people.

The first means nothing without the second two elements. Thus, it was not by accident that the framers of the Constitution put freedom of expression as the First Amendment to the Bill of Rights. Nations may have all

1

the free elections they want but unless their citizens are truly informed, those elections are largely meaningless. No citizen can adequately judge the performance of his leaders unless he has sufficient facts on which to make an informed judgment.

In dictatorships, the few who rule the many are removed only by death, some form of coup, or revolution. In democracies, the few who govern must account to the electorate—whether the news is good or bad—and then regularly submit themselves to the people's judgment at the polls. It is this ultimate judgment that alone determines whether governmental power will be continued or taken away. Of course, there is no guarantee that the people will make the correct decision. There is only the hope that they will do so. But in order to properly judge the standards of governmental actions, the citizenry must be able to obtain, at their will, knowledge about the activities and workings of the government. In short, to quote John Philpot Curran, "Eternal vigilance is the price of liberty."

Regrettably, throughout our 200-year history, our First Amendment guarantees—the "people's right to know"—have been blocked by the great brick wall of government silence and secrecy. Until 1967, public entry to records and documents held by the Federal government was governed by a "need to know" policy, stemming from the 1789 "housekeeping" law, which gave Federal agencies the right to authorize the withholding of information from the public; and from a provision of the Administrative Procedure Act of 1946, which stated that matters of official note should be made available to the public, but added that an agency could limit entry to its papers "for good cause found" or "in the public interest."

The Freedom of Information Act, adopted in 1966 and made effective in 1967, reversed this policy and the seeds of a new era of openness were planted. It gave us rights we thought we already had. But it was not comprehensive enough. So in 1974 a series of needed amendments were tacked on. In the Senate, Edward M. Kennedy of Massachusetts spoke of a "hostile bureaucracy" and acclaimed the bill as one of the positive legacies of the Watergate era.

The decision as to how a document will be classified (Top Secret, Secret, Limited Official Use, Confidential, Eyes Only, etc.) is too often taken by an official for the wrong reasons. And Uncle Sam has been snooping too much and telling too little for too long. Armed with these new legal longbows to combat excessive Federal secrecy, Americans have begun to win some battles.

The target objective: the swollen files in which Federal agencies maintain billions of classified papers, running the gamut from sensitive national security information to detailed reports on unsuspecting citizens placed under the eye of Big Brother because they attended protest marches, political rallies and radical—and not so radical—activities.

No one seems to be above suspicion. When Bella Abzug was serving as a Democratic Representative from New York she asked the CIA what it had on her. To her surprise she found out that for 22 years the CIA—an organization charged with overseas intelligence gathering as it concerns national security—had been monitoring her activities as a lawyer and politician.

Democratic Representative Charles Porter from Oregon cast a line out to the CIA and caught 17 items in a dossier, including a report on his attendance at a 1968 conference of the Congress of Racial Equality in Oakland, California. Porter was reported to have asked: "What the hell does that have to do with the CIA? They're treating me like a security risk?"

A closely guarded secret for years, cable traffic relating

to the annual foreign travel of the 435 members of Congress and 100 Senators can now be pried loose from the State Department and the Pentagon. Columnist Jack Anderson has done numerous columns on the freeloading and high living by our legislators. He revealed, for example, that the State Department had shipped home carpeting that the wife of New Mexico Senator Joseph Montoya had purchased during a visit to Hong Kong.

The Washington *Post* got the State Department to open its files on the official foreign gifts to former President Nixon and his family. Seventeen thousand pages of research and other materials that the Department of the Army had withheld on the My Lai massacre were given sunlight by the Oklahoma City *Daily Oklahoman.*

Brothers Robert and Michael Meeropol have been using the Freedom of Information Act to break loose documents from the FBI and CIA that they believe will ultimately clear their parents' names, Julius and Ethel Rosenberg, the couple put to death as nuclear spies in 1953.

Operating on the principle that sunlight is the best disinfectant, I have written this book. It is not my fear that members of the Cosa Nostra will use it to obtain information from the FBI on how it combats organized crime. I don't worry that KGB agents will use it to get national security or defense secrets. Fears such as these are baseless, as it seems inconceivable that our courts would ever demand that the agencies release information that could in any way endanger law enforcement investigatory methods or the defense of our country.

But it's because of a Freedom of Information lawsuit that the FBI is spewing forth tens of thousands of pages concerning its investigation of the President John F. Kennedy assassination. Thanks to this Act we now know about multitudes of malversations at the highest levels of government. A special body of secret law at the Federal Trade Commission was made public, Alger Hiss's celebrated "Pumpkin Papers" reached the surface, and Central Intelligence Agency documents highlighting its domestic and overseas assassinations were made public.

The requests come in by the tens of thousands and cover a wide range of government activities. It has been reported that the General Services Administration—in a sense Uncle's landlord—was asked for the exact count on how much toilet paper it purchases every year for the supersecret National Security Agency.

While some of the requests may seem frivolous to many people, they serve to keep our countrymen—those who sit in a public trust—on guard and looking out for our best interests, we hope. If we do not exercise our rights and the few are adroit in their serpentine maneuverings—via propaganda, secrecy, distortions, omissions and outright lies— they can hold the reins of government for years, even decades and, in some cases, generations. To further quote the Honorable John E. Moss, "A democracy without a free and truthful flow of information from government to its people is nothing more than an elected dictatorship. We can never permit this to happen in America."

In the preparation of this book I've made every effort to present sound, carefully documented data and, at the same time, to present the Freedom of Information Act in simple, direct language so that it might be read and understood by the greatest number.

The Freedom of Information Act is not the end-all and cure-all. While it's producing many surprises, Washington still has a penchant for secrecy. Agencies are forever seeking new ways to block the Act and thwart sneak attacks on their heavy concrete and marble fortresses. Officials still believe in a "territorial imperative."

Regardless of the fact that the Act is burdensome to bureaucracy and costly to the citizenry, and is abused in abundance, it saps government's power to cover its errors with a classification stamp and ink pad. Watergate taught us all how Executive government used "national security" to justify illegal wiretaps and scores of other improper activities.

It is with this in mind that I have attempted here to reduce the Freedom of Information Act to a form and format which is understandable and useable.

"The mutual confidence on which all else depends can be maintained only by an open mind and a brave reliance on free discussion."—Judge Learned Hand (1872-1961).

CHAPTER 1

The History of the Act

"Enduring governments must be accountable to someone besides themselves."—WALTER LIPPMANN

The Freedom of Information Act (FOIA) was signed into law by President Lyndon B. Johnson on July 4, 1966, as Public Law 89-487. It went into effect on July 4, 1967. In his bill-signing statement President Johnson said:

This legislation springs from one of our most essential principles: a democracy works best when the people have all the information that the security of the Nation permits. No one should be able to pull the curtains of secrecy around decisions which can be revealed without injury to the public interest. . . . I signed this measure with a deep sense of pride that the United States is an open society in which the people's right to know is cherished and guarded.

Attorney General Ramsey Clark said at the time: "If government is to be truly of, by, and for the people, the people must know in detail the activities of government. Nothing so diminishes democracy as secrecy."

The new law followed more than a decade of effort on its behalf by the Foreign Operations and Government Information Subcommittee and its predecessor, the Special Subcommittee on Government Information, established on June 9, 1955, under the chairmanship of Representative John E. Moss of California. Similar efforts were focused in the Senate Subcommittee on Administration Practice and Procedure, under the chairmanship of Senator Edward V. Long of Missouri, and its parent Committee on the Judiciary. Volumes of hearings, investigations, and studies of information policies of the Federal Government over this 11-year period produced a myriad of reports, committee prints and analyses of the withholding of information by the Executive bureaucracy.

Then in 1958, near the end of the 85th Congress, the House and Senate enacted, without a dissenting vote, the first statute devoted solely to freedom of information. The Moss bill (H.R. 2767) was a one sentence amendment to the 1789 "housekeeping" law which gave Federal agencies the authority to regulate the business of the agencies and to set up filing systems and keep records. The language of the amendment added to section 22 of title 5 of the United States Code was:

"This section does not authorize withholding information from the public or limiting the availability of records to the public."

Yet in 1972 hearings before the subcommittee indicate that some agencies were still relying on the original 1789 "housekeeping" statute as authority to withhold certain types of information from the public, despite the enactment of Public Law 85-619 fourteen years before.

The Freedom of Information Act was enacted as an amendment of section 3 of the Administrative Procedure Act of 1946 and emerged from the functional inadequacy of the prior section 3, which contained the first general statutory provision for public disclosure of executive branch rules, opinions, and orders, and public records. Many of its provisions, however, were vague and contained disabling loopholes which made the section as much a basis for withholding information as one for disclosing. Section 3 as originally enacted was the target of many legislative attempts to close the loopholes and make the language more specific, but all failed of final approval until the 1966 amendment.

The Freedom of Information Act was a milestone legislation that reversed long-standing Government information policies and customs. Previously, most agencies operated on the basis of section 3 of the Administrative Procedure Act of 1946 which stated that unless otherwise required by statute, "matters of official record shall in accordance with published rule be made available to persons properly and directly concerned except information held confidential for good cause found." It was the perfect out for Uncle Sam. Moreover, the original section 3 contained a blanket exclusion from its applicability of any function of the United States requiring secrecy in the "public interest" and "any matter relating solely to the internal management of any agency."

The Freedom of Information Act replaced this general language relating to secrecy, indicating that Congress, in enacting the FOIA, has adopted a policy that "any person" should have clear access to identifiable agency records without having to state a reason for wanting the information and that the burden of proving withholding to be necessary is placed on the Federal agency.

In order to withhold information Government must justify its decision on the basis of one of nine specific exemptions permitted in the act. These exemptions will be discussed in Chapter 3, "The Nine Exemptions."

But after all this the law didn't work. It contained no deadlines for compliance and no penal ties for violation. With few exceptions, the federal bureaucratic machine answered by delay in processing requests, obfuscation, excessive fees for copying and searching for documents, and other roadblocks. It was reported that some critics began calling it a "freedom *from* information" law.

The House Foreign Operations and Government Information Subcommittee held 14 days of oversight hearings in the 92nd Congress relating to the administration of the Freedom of Information Act by Federal agencies, following which the House Subcommittee identified six "major problem areas":

1. The bureaucratic delay in responding to an individual's request for information—major Federal agencies took an average of 33 days with such responses; and when acting upon an appeal from a decision to deny the information, major agencies took an average of 50 additional days;

2. The abuses in fee schedules by some agencies for searching and copying of documents and records requested by individuals; excessive charges for such services have been an effective bureaucratic tool in denying information to individual requestors;

3. The cumbersome and costly legal remedy under the act when persons denied information by an agency choose to invoke the injunctive procedures to obtain access; although the private person has prevailed over the Government bureaucracy a majority of the important cases under

the act that have gone to the Federal courts, the time it takes, the investment of many thousands of dollars in attorney fees and court costs, and the advantages to the Government in such cases makes litigation under the act less than feasible in many situations;

4. The lack of involvement in the decision-making process by public information officials when information is denied to an individual making a request under the act; most agencies provide for little or no input from the public information specialists and the key decisions are made by political appointees—general counsels, assistant secretaries, or other top-echelon officials;

5. The relative lack of utilization of the act by the news media, which had been among the strongest backers of the freedom of information legislation prior to its enactment; the time factor is a significant reason because of the more urgent need for information by the media to meet news deadlines. The delaying tactics of the Federal bureaucrats are a major deterrent to more widespread use of the act, although the subcommittee did receive testimony from several reporters and editors who have taken cases to court and eventually won out over the secrecy-minded Government bureaucracy; and

6. The lack of priority given by top-level administrators to the full implementation and proper enforcement of Freedom of Information Act policies and regulations; a more positive attitude in support of "open access" from the top administrative officials is needed throughout the executive branch. In too many cases, information is withheld, overclassified, or otherwise hidden from the public to avoid administrative mistakes, waste of funds, or political embarrassment. In Washington this is known as "dynamic inaction" whereby keeping things from happening the bureaucrat prevents mistakes from being made.

In 1974 Congress attempted again to plug some of these most obvious loopholes. It offered a series of amendments which covered the areas of index publication, record identification, search and copying fees, court review, response to complaints, expedited appeals, assessment of attorney fees and costs, sanction, administrative deadlines, national defense and foreign policy exemptions, annual reports by agencies, segregable portions of records and expansion of agency definition.

These areas were amended essentially as follows:*

INDEX PUBLICATION

It was agreed that the Freedom of Information law would require each agency to publish and distribute (by sale or otherwise) indexes identifying information for the public as to any matter issued, adopted or promulgated after July 4, 1967. This includes final options, orders, agency statements of policy and interpretations not published in the *Federal Register,* and administrative staff manuals and agency staff instructions that affect the public unless they are otherwise published and offered for sale to the public. Further the publication of such indexes should be on a quarterly or more frequent basis. And if an agency determines not to publish its index, it shall provide copies on request to any person at a cost not to exceed the direct cost of duplication.

IDENTIFIABLE RECORDS

It was agreed that the request only "reasonably describe" the records being sought.

* For precise wording see the full text of the Freedom of Information Act, as amended in 1974 by Public Law 93-502.

SEARCH AND COPYING FEES

It was agreed that each agency would be required to issue its own regulations for the recovery of only the direct costs of search and duplication—not to include examination or review of records. And if an agency could furnish the records requested without charge or at a reduced rate, it should do so if it determined that such action would be in the public interest.

COURT REVIEW

It was agreed that in determining *de novo* whether agency records have been properly withheld, the court may examine records *in camera* in making its determination under any of the nine categories of exemptions.

RESPONSE TO COMPLAINTS

It was agreed to give the defendant 30 days to respond, unless the court directs otherwise for good cause shown.

EXPEDITED APPEALS

It was agreed to give precedence on appeal to cases brought under the Freedom of Information law, except as to cases on the docket which the court considers of greater importance.

ASSESSMENT OF ATTORNEY FEES AND COSTS

It was agreed that a Federal court may, in its discretion, assess reasonable attorney fees and other litigation costs reasonably incurred by the complainant in Freedom of Information cases in which the Federal government has not prevailed.

SANCTION

It was agreed that in a Freedom of Information case, the court could impose a sanction of up to 60 days suspension from employment against a Federal employee or official when the circumstances surrounding the withholding raise questions whether agency personnel acted arbitrarily or capriciously with respect to the withholding. If the Court so finds, the Civil Service Commission must immediately initiate a proceeding to determine whether disciplinary action is warranted against the responsible officer or employee. This section applies to all persons employed by agencies under this law.

ADMINISTRATIVE DEADLINES

It was agreed to generally adopt 10- to 20-day administrative deadlines with a 10-working-day extension for "unusual circumstances" in situations where the agency must search for and collect the requested records from facilities separate from the office processing the request, where the agency must search for, collect, and examine a voluminous amount of separate and distinct records demanded in a single request, or where the agency has a need to consult with another agency or agency unit having substantial interest in the determination because of the subject matter. This 10-day extension may be invoked only once by the agency—either during initial review of the request or during appellate review.

NATIONAL DEFENSE AND FOREIGN POLICY EXEMPTION

It was agreed that withholding of information would be permitted where it is "specifically authorized under criteria established by an Executive order to be kept secret in the interest of national defense or foreign policy" and is "in fact, properly classified" pursuant to both procedural and substantive criteria contained in such Executive order.

INVESTIGATORY RECORDS

It was agreed that an agency could withhold investigatory records compiled for law enforcement purposes only to the extent that the production of such records would interfere with enforcement proceedings, deprive a person of a right to fair trial or an impartial adjudication, constitute an unwarranted invasion of personal privacy, disclose the identity of a confidential source, disclose investigative techniques and procedures or endanger the life or physical safety of law enforcement personnel.

SEGREGABLE PORTIONS OF RECORDS

It was agreed that any reasonably segregable portion of a record shall be provided to any person requesting such record after the deletion of portions which may be exempted under subsection (b) of the Freedom of Information law.

ANNUAL REPORTS BY AGENCIES

It was agreed that each agency must submit an annual report, on or before March 1 of each calendar year, to the Speaker of the House and the President of the Senate, for referral to the appropriate committees of the Congress.

The report should contain: statistical information on the number of agency determinations to withhold information requested under the FOIA; the reasons for such withholdings; the numbers of appeals of such adverse determinations with the result and reasons for each; a copy of every rule made by the agency in connection with this law; a copy of the agency fee schedule with the total amount of fees collected by the agency during the year; a list of those officials responsible for each denial of records and the number of cases in which each participated during the year; a full report from the Attorney General on or before March 1 of each calendar year listing the number of cases arising under the Freedom of Information law, the exemption involved in each such case, the disposition of the case, and the costs, fees, and penalties assessed under the law, and other information indicating efforts to properly administer the Freedom of Information law (in the case of the Attorney General, his report must include a description of the Department of Justice's efforts to encourage agency compliance with the law).

EXPANSION OF AGENCY DEFINITION

It was agreed that the Freedom of Information law would include any executive department, military department, Government corporation, Government-controlled corporation, or other establishment in the executive branch of Government (including the Executive Office of the President), or any independent regulatory agency.

In the debate that transpired the attitude taken by the majority of the Representatives is summed up by a statement by Dante B. Fascell, a member of the Committee on Governmental Operations:

"Mr. Chairman, one historical reference is particularly important in understanding the need for these amendments. When hearings were held nine years ago by the Moss subcommittee on legislation that finally was enacted as the Freedom of Information Act of 1966, every single witness from the Federal bureaucracy—then under a Democratic President—opposed the bill. They claimed that it would seriously hamper the functioning of Federal agencies and be ruinous to the decisionmaking process. Despite their opposition, the bill was unanimously passed by the Congress and President Johnson wisely signed it into law. Of course, no such calamitous result was forthcoming. The spectres never appeared. During the hearings on this current legislation to strengthen the freedom of information law, every single witness from the Federal bureaucracy—this time under a Republican President—has again opposed the bill, using the same types of discredited arguments heard nine years ago. I trust that history will repeat itself and that Congress will again give its overwhelming approval to freedom of information legislation and that the present White House incumbent will likewise sign the bill into law."

This was not to happen. The suggestion of freedom of information amendments brought the Federal bureaucrats down on the White House like Popski's Private Army.

His pledges of an "open" administration notwithstanding, President Ford vetoed the bill straightaway. In a letter to the House of Representatives, dated October 17, 1974, he concluded, "It is only my conviction that the bill as enrolled is unconstitutional and unworkable that would cause me to return the bill without my approval. I sincerely hope that this legislation, which has come so far toward realizing its laudable goals, will be reenacted with the changes I propose and returned to me for signature during this session of Congress."

It never happened. In the face of Watergate and other assorted government transgressions that had been kept *sub rosa*, the amended Freedom of Information Act was passed over his veto. The vote went as follows: House of Representatives, yeas 65, nays 31, not voting 32; Senate, yeas 65, nays 27, not voting 8. The amended law became effective February 19, 1975.

Senator Ted Kennedy of Massachusetts perhaps said it best: "Secret government too easily advances narrow interests at the expense of the public interest." He further reemphasized the importance to democracy of a free flow of information from government to the public:

> We should keep in mind that it does not take marching armies to end republics. Superior firepower may preserve tyrannies, but it is not necessary to create them. If the people of a democratic nation do not know what decisions their government is making, do not know the basis on which those decisions are being made, then their rights as a free people may gradually slip away, silently stolen when decisions which affect their lives are made under the cover of secrecy.

The Freedom of Information Act is the product of great thought, debate, and consideration. Its regulations adhere closely to the philosophy of the public's right to know the business of its Government.

Attorney General Ramsey Clark, in issuing the overall guidance to executive agencies for their administration of the Freedom of Information Act, said: "Self-government, the maximum participation of the citizenry in affairs of state, is meaningful only with an informed public. How can we govern ourselves if we know not how we govern? Never was it more important than in our times of mass society, when government affects each individual in so many ways, that the right of the people to know the actions of their government be secure."

CHAPTER 2

How to Invoke the Act

"With the people and their representatives reduced to a state of ignorance, the democratic process is paralyzed."—
JUSTICE POTTER STEWART

Since literally every member of the Federal bureaucracy is familiar with the Freedom of Information Act and its import, it is usually worthwhile to make an informal attempt at getting the documents you want before starting the formal "paper chase" under the Act. I have found that many bureaucrats have been ordered to avoid requests under the Freedom of Information Act wherever and whenever possible. Thus, when you first go into an agency looking for specific information, steer clear of the FOI Officer and go directly to the official with the most authority over the documents you desire. In this way you may be pleasantly surprised to find that the documents are released immediately without a fight or that they are already cleared for public examination.

An informal preliminary request can be most beneficial

19

to you in the area of identifying the actual documents you want. The law says that you must "reasonably describe" the records you want under the Freedom of Information Act. It is during an informal telephone request that you may be able to get the bureaucrat to slip with the name of the documents you seek. Such information can help you avoid further delays when your ultimate request under the Act is made.

Throughout your informal effort and at all future stages, keep detailed notes on your telephone conversations and on any personal visits with agency officials. Needless to say, copies of all correspondence should be made.

REVIEW THE REGULATIONS

Prior to making your formal request, go over the regulations governing the use of the Act. You'll have to follow to a "T" the particulars set forth. If you try and cut corners or get sloppy, the agency may be able to slip out from under the Act and not consider it within the FOIA's rigid time limits. Your request could easily fall into some fathomless bureaucratic abyss never to be found. "It fell through the cracks" is a common cry in Washington, D.C. It seems at times that professional bureaucrats operate on the basis of staunch decision postponement and non-responsiveness wherever and whenever possible. Don't give them the chance!

THE REQUEST

You do not need the formal name of the document or report but you must describe it well enough so that it can be found with a reasonable try. Give all the details you can.

The request should be addressed to the agency having the records, its general counsel or the agency official designated to handle FOI Act matters. Slug the request letter and its envelope with "Freedom of Information Act Request/Do Not Delay." Give your telephone number in the letter to speed things up.

Remember: If your request arrives at the wrong office it will be forwarded and the agency's time limit does not begin until it reaches the proper office.

At major agencies that are centralized like the Federal Bureau of Investigation this should not pose a problem, but misdirection could cause aggravating delays at agencies spread out across the nation like the United States Immigration and Naturalization Service.

INS processes an average of 90,000 formal requests for records each year, seeking access to one or more of the 12 million individual files dispersed and frequently transfered between 57 widely scattered service offices and 10 Federal record centers.

FEES

The law allows the government to assess "reasonable standard charges for document search and duplication." It says these fees may be waived if the agency decides that release of the information primarily benefits the public-at-large. *You could save money by asking to see the documents instead of having copies made.* Your request may set a limit on such charges in advance. (See "Sample Request.")

These charges vary from several cents a page to 25¢ per page. Many agencies will not charge you if the copying expense is less than $3.00, but others have minimum fee schedules.

Most agencies cannot charge you for the time its lawyers and other officials spend researching your request. However, some have a flat hourly rate. It pays to read the agency's regulations before making a request.

If you feel the release of certain documents will benefit the public interest, make this argument in your letter of request. The agencies are allowed to make such public interest decisions on a case-by-case basis.

TIMETABLE

A request for information must be answered within 10 working days (not including Saturdays, Sundays and holidays). If some or all of the requested material is denied, you *must* be informed of your right to appeal and provided with the name of the official, usually the agency's director, who will rule on it. With some exemptions, that decision *must* be made within 20 working days from the time the appeal is filed.

APPEALS

Here, again, the agency rules will tell you in detail precisely how to address the appeal so that it gets to the proper office. Slug the request letter and its envelope: "Freedom of Information Act Appeal/Do Not Delay."

If you lose the appeal or there is no response within the prescribed periods, you may file suit in Federal court where you live, where the agency records are held, or in the District of Columbia. The court will consider the entire matter *de novo;* i.e., the court can make a new determination pursuant to the Act. THE BURDEN OF PROOF IS ON THE AGENCY. The court may ask to inspect the document itself.

How long will such a case take? The Act stipulates that

FOI appeals should be given every priority on court dockets and "expedited in every way."

In a win will you recover court costs? The Act specifies that the court may assess lawyers' fees and other litigation expenses in cases against the government where you "substantially prevail."

When facing a suit in Federal court, the government must file an answer in 30 days, instead of the customary 60 days, unless they win a delay by proving "exceptional circumstances."

The Central Intelligence Agency, for example, has been asked for the records of "all expenditures" since the Agency was formed in 1948. The request was turned down and now sits in the courts. This, needless to say, is an "exceptional circumstance."

However, the State Department was forced to reveal "background" briefings on President Ford's meeting in Vladivostok with the U.S.S.R.'s Leonid Brezhnev.

SAMPLE REQUEST

(Name and Address of Government Agency)
Washington, D.C. Zip Code

Re: A Freedom of Information Request

Dear (general counsel or other designated official):

Pursuant to the Freedom of Information Act, 5 U.S.C. 552, I hereby request access to, or a copy of (describe the document), together with all appendices, annexes, or other materials attached to (document).

If any expenses in excess of $_____ are incurred in connection with this request, please inform me in advance for my approval. (You may ask that any fees be waived if furnishing the information could be considered as "primarily benefitting the public.")

If you determine that some portions of the (document) are exempt from release, I request that you provide me with the remainder. I hereby reserve my right to appeal any such decisions.

If you do not grant this request within 10 working days, I will consider my request denied. If you should wish to discuss the matter, my telephone number is (Area Code + ———).

Thanking you in advance for your time and consideration, I am,

Sincerely,

SOURCES OF ASSISTANCE

After reading this book, if you need further assistance in exercising your rights under the FOI Act, you might contact:

The Reporters Committee for Freedom of the Press
Room 1112
1750 Pennsylvania Avenue, N.W.
Washington, D.C. 20006
Tel: (202) 298-7460

Freedom of Information Clearing House
2000 P Street, N.W.
Washington, D.C. 20036
Tel: (202) 785-3407

Freedom of Information Center
School of Journalism

P.O. Box 858
University of Missouri
Columbia, Missouri 65201
Tel: (314) 882-4856

Project on Freedom of Information and the National
Security*
122 Maryland Avenue, N.E.
Washington, D.C. 20002
Tel: (202) 544-5380

FURTHER BACKGROUND

For additional detailed discussion of the Act, you might
acquire:

1) "The Freedom of Information Act: A Seven Year
Assessment," Vol. 74, *Columbia Law Review*—begin at page
895 (June, 1974).

2) "Symposium on the 1974 Amendments to the Freedom of Information Act," Vol. 25, *The American University
Law Review*—begin at page 1 (Fall, 1975).

3) *Freedom of Information Act and Amendments of 1974 (P.L.
93-502),* published by the Committee on Government
Operations, U.S. House of Representatives, and the Committee on the Judiciary, U.S. Senate, for sale by the Superintendent of Documents, U.S. Government Printing
Office, Washington, D.C. 20402. Price $4.80. Catalog
Number Y4. G74/7: IN3/16.

4) *Attorney General's Memorandum on the 1974 Amendments*

* This is sponsored jointly by the American Civil Liberties Union
Foundation and the Center for National Security Studies. It is
operated by Morton Halperin, a former National Security Council
aide. *Specialization:* Documents held by the Defense Department,
Central Intelligence Agency, State Department and National Security Council.

to the Freedom of Information Act, published by the United States Department of Justice, available from the Superintendent of Documents, U.S. Government Printing Office, Washington, D.C. 20402. Price 90¢. Catalog Number j 1.2: IN3/974.

CHAPTER 3

The Nine Exemptions

"It is not providence on Mount Sinai that stamps a document secret or top secret, but a lot of boys and girls just like us who have all their own hangups."—U.S. SENATOR JACOB K. JAVITZ

Striving for a *workable balance* between the right of the people to know and the need of the Government to keep information in confidence to the extent necessary without permitting indiscriminate secrecy, the Freedom of Information Act contains a set of nine exemptions.

The nine exemptions in the Act which permit withholding of information have been misused by Federal agencies. Confused interpretations of agency regulations, the desire to withhold records which might embarrass an agency, and the misunderstanding of court decisions affecting these exemptions, all have contributed to the problem.

Make sure you understand these nine exemptions prior to making a request. But don't let them completely influence your decision to proceed with a particular request.

27

Don't forget that while the government *may* withhold information from you if it is so justified under any of the nine specific exemptions permitted in the Act, the withholding of information under the Freedom of Information Act is discretionary, not mandatory. Therefore, I emphasize the word *may*. Agencies usually honor the requests if they want to; the Act only limits the circumstances under which the agencies decide *not* to make documents available.

Exemption One

(A) Matters that are specifically authorized under criteria established by an Executive order to be kept secret in the interest of national defense or foreign policy and (B) are in fact properly classified pursuant to such Executive order.

The key words here are "properly classified." If you make a request for documents which an agency has stamped SECRET in the interest of national defense or foreign policy, the agency *must* re-review these records and make a determination as to whether or not the records you've asked for warrant continued classification under the criteria of the Executive order governing the protection of national security information, the age of the document notwithstanding. Therefore, it is conceivable that a request to inspect records which were classified SECRET several years ago may set off a re-examination of that classification resulting in public availability of the documents.

If you feel that certain documents should not be kept from you under this exemption, don't forget that under the 1974 amendments the Federal courts may examine a claim of national security to see if it is being used to suppress material that would be politically embarrassing but not truly sensitive.

Also, proper classification of a few pages of a report *does not* justify secrecy for the entire document. Pages, paragraphs, even sentences must be made public if they are at all intelligible, according to the Justice Department.

Exemption Two

Matters that are related solely to the internal personnel rules and practices of an agency.

This exemption covers such materials as manuals that relate only to internal management and organization of an agency, but would not exempt staff manuals instructing Federal employees on how to perform their jobs or descriptions of these jobs. The courts have interpreted this exemption strictly (see *Vaughn v. Rosen*, 523 F.2d 1136 - D.C. Cir. 1975). Interestingly enough, some examples of materials which an agency can withhold under this exemption include lunch schedules, parking regulations, and sick-leave policies.

Exemption Three

Matters that are specifically exempted from disclosure by statute.

There are more than 100 deferral statutes which permit agencies to withhold from disclosure certain records or documents. Examples of documents which are kept confidential include income tax returns, applications for patents and completed census forms.

However, it is doubtful if any such statutes composed after the enactment of the Freedom of Information Act will present a problem since they were written with a full understanding of the Act and its allowance for other specific statutory exemptions. Your problems will be more apt to occur when dealing with statutes written prior to the Freedom of Information Act which, in general terms, permit or demand that an agency withhold certain documents and records.

The poser then is whether the exemption in the Freedom of Information Act for records "specifically exempted from disclosure by statute" will permit an agency to withhold documents based upon a general statute such as that which permits an agency to hold back documents "deemed confidential."

While the courts have yielded to the other statutes (see *FAA v. Robertson*, 422 U.S. 255 - 1975), legislation has been introduced which would mention explicitly that general statutes would be ruled by the standards in the Freedom of Information Act rather than permitting the agencies to wield blanket-type discretion as presently seems to be the case.

EXEMPTION FOUR

Matters that are trade secrets and commercial or financial information obtained from a person and privileged or confidential.

Material falling under this exemption must consist of trade secrets or commercial or financial information, *and* must have been obtained from a person—not a government agency—*and* must be privileged or confidential. Here once again one is dealing with how "privileged or confidential" is interpreted.

EXEMPTION FIVE

Matters that are inter-agency or intra-agency memorandums or letters which would not be available by law to a party other than an agency in litigation with the agency.

This has been a widely used exemption and much litigation has taken place over it. Government agencies seem to be quick to claim that documents are "intra-agency memoranda." The courts have supported agency use of this exemption when the documents carry views and recommendations of officials on policy or legal matters, when they are part of the "deliberative process." On the other hand, experts suggest it does not apply to factual reports or analyses—even though a document might have been written by staffers solely for the use of that agency.

It becomes sticky for the agency when a factual report is incapable of being disentangled from official recommendations—the "deliberative process"; then the agency may get away with a nondisclosure position. For example, a memorandum from a staff chemist to his supervisor concerning his opinions on a specific drug or an official suggesting certain action in a case pending at the FCC would be exempt from public disclosure. However, those portions of the memorandum listing facts—for example, in the case of the chemist, perhaps the program under which the drug was submitted, or, in the case of the FCC, an analysis of facts relating to television signal transmission—would be public information.

But watch out here because it can get tricky. It is very possible under this exemption that an agency will state that a certain decision or recommendation of a lesser body working within or under the agency's umbrella is an "intra-agency memorandum" and, therefore, exempt from disclosure. Now the question comes up as to whether the lesser body alone is an "agency" and, thus, subject to the Act, although even if it is the records in case might be considered "inter-agency." However, remember that if an agency takes on specific recommendations made by the lesser body then it is considered a "final agency decision" and, thereby, available for public inspection and copying, according to law (522 (a) (2) (A)).

The second part of Exemption Five suggests that if an inter-agency or intra-agency document is made available to a private party engaged in litigation with the agency, then it should be available for public disclosure. In this instance, you will need some understanding of the Federal Rules of Civil Procedures and its Rules of Discovery. Basically, under the Rules of Discovery, documents become available when you demonstrate need. With the straight Freedom of Information Act no motive or need is usually required.

EXEMPTION SIX

Matters that deal with personnel and medical files and similar files the disclosure of which would constitute a clearly unwarranted invasion of personal privacy.

This sounds at first reading like an impossible one to break but some determination is needed. If your request touches this area, you should explain why you want the information so that the officials can weigh whether any invasion of privacy resulting from disclosure would be "unwarranted."

Here are two examples of just how this exemption works in practice. There were once two law professors, who were studying the labor vote and needed the names and addresses of specific union employees eligible to vote in representation elections. The court, in this case, felt that the public would benefit in the long run from the scholars' work, compared to the slight invasion into the privacy of those workers listed. Their request did not establish a "clearly unwarranted invasion of personal privacy." For the full details you may wish to search *Getman v. NLRB,* 450 F.2d 670 (DC Cir. 1971).

However, in *Winehobby U.S.A., Inc.* v. *Bureau of Alcohol,*

Tobacco and Firearms, 502 F.2d 133 (3rd Cir. 1974), a distributor of wine-making gear wanted from a Federal agency a complete listing of all the names and addresses of all amateur winemakers filing for tax-exempt status. The judge ruled that Winehobby U.S.A., Inc., had obvious commercial interests (i.e., selling its wine-making products) and this did not exceed the invasion of privacy that would result to citizens from the public disclosure of their names and addresses. It had, in fact, tried to get a mailing list made up of a highly targeted audience from the government—at no cost.

Exemption Seven

Matters that are investigatory records compiled for law enforcement purposes, but only to the extent that the production of such records would (A) interfere with enforcement proceedings, (B) deprive a person of a right to a fair trial or an impartial adjudication, (C) constitute an unwarranted invasion of personal privacy, (D) disclose the identity of a confidential source and, in the case of a record compiled by a criminal law enforcement authority in the course of a criminal investigation; or by an agency conducting a lawful national security intelligence investigation, confidential information furnished only by the confidential source, (E) disclose investigative techniques and procedures, or (F) endanger the life or physical safety of law enforcement personnel.

Before the 1974 revision of this exemption, agencies regularly held back disclosures of documents by claiming they were "investigatory files." As you can see, this has changed. Today the Government must prove that 1) the records requested are in fact investigatory documents compiled for law enforcement purposes, and 2) that release would involve one of the six types of injuries broken out in clauses (A) thru (F) as cited above.

EXEMPTION EIGHT

Matters contained in or related to examination, operating, or condition reports prepared by, on behalf of, or for the use of an agency responsible for the regulation or supervision of financial institutions.

This refers to reports prepared by or for an agency responsible for the supervision of financial institutions, such as reports by the Securities and Exchange Commission on the New York Stock Exchange.

EXEMPTION NINE

Matters involving geological and geophysical information and data, including maps, concerning wells.

This would include, for example, information on hand involving the oil and natural gas explorations by private firms.

But to some government agencies even these nine exemptions don't provide enough "out" for them. Behind the scenes there is a movement to restore secrecy in Washington, D.C.

To date there have been no major legislative inroads on the disclosure laws established under the FOIA and its amendments. Senator Edward Kennedy and his Senate Judiciary Subcommittee on Administrative Practice and Procedure keep a constant vigil.

It has been reported that the Parole Commission attempted to circumnavigate the Act by re-writing the federal parole procedures. Hidden inside the revision was a brief statement that Sections 551 through 559 of Title 5 of the U.S. Code "shall not apply" to the Commission's work.

On the surface this appears innocent, but Section 552 is

the Freedom of Information Act and Section 552-A is the Privacy Act. Senator Kennedy and his crack staff caught the proposed bill after it had already been passed intact by the House. Needless to say, the passage was deleted.

In a tête-à-tête with the Transportation Safety Board in 1975, Senator Kennedy said that he would continue to "oppose attempts to circumvent the Freedom of Information Act with provisions vague in language, overbroad in scope, or unjustified by clearly evidenced need."

The Kennedy confrontation with the Safety Board was over the so-called "Chicago Convention," an international pact which cautions against the release of specific aircraft accident data put together during inquiries led by foreign governments.

The catalyzer was a protest by the French government that the Transportation Safety Board might not be able to maintain the confidentiality of information in adequate fashion.

The way the Safety Board had originally submitted the bill, not even the U.S. courts would have been able to break the information loose. It afforded such files absolute secrecy from everybody.

The way it read, only the foreign nations, the Safety Board and the aircraft manufacturers were entitled to the information; these are the groups which normally might participate in a crash investigation. But the passengers and their families who might be suing for damages were left out in the cold. In fact, so was Congress!

After some negotiation the bill was trimmed of its excessive roadblocks—allowed to protect only "confidential information"—and then only at the precise appeal of a foreign state, and for a maximum of two years. It then passed the Senate.

Agencies are forever trying to slip the noose of freedom

of information. But Congress is serious about letting sunlight enter and it maintains an eagle eye on behalf of the
taxpayers. Every time an agency submits a bill that might
give it a loophole in the Act, Congress amends it or otherwise thwarts the action.

However, in all of this there is another problem; more
laws go on the books. According to statistics compiled by a
House Government Operations subcommittee, more than
70 such laws are now on the books. Unfortunately, more
seem likely to come.

There are certain agency favorites. The CIA pulls out
its power to protect "intelligence sources and methods
from unauthorized disclosure." The Postal Service relishes
the law allowing secrecy for "the reports and memoranda
of consultants or independent contractors." Agriculture
clings to the statute directing confidentiality for the reports submitted by "warehousemen, processors and common carriers of corn, wheat, cotton, rice, peanuts or
tobacco . . . all ginners of cotton . . . all brokers and
dealers in peanuts" and similar etceteras.

One congressional staffer feels that it's better to have
many individually fashioned statutes than to survey new
and broader exemptions.

It may never be easy for our bureaucrats to be totally
comfortable with freedom of information. Nor may it ever
be for our elected officials. One CIA official is quoted as
saying, "They teach you here for 20 years how to keep information secret and inside the Company. Then the Hill
comes along and tells us to do an aboutface, review what
can go out, and make it public." Elected officials are still
haunted by Watergate and the assorted kick-back
schemes, pay-offs and indictments.

Understand what you may be up against concerning
the nine exemptions and the other laws that have been

tacked on. However, do not let any of them deter you from your quest. Perhaps Justice Brandeis stated best the significant purpose behind the Freedom of Information Act when he wrote:

"Publicity is justly commendable as a remedy for social and industrial disease. Sunlight is said to be the best disinfectant, and electric light the most effective policeman."

REMEMBER!! ANY REASONABLE SEGREGABLE POR-TION OF A RECORD MUST BE PROVIDED TO YOU AFTER THE DELETIONS OF THE PORTIONS WHICH ARE EXEMPT UNDER THIS SUBSECTION.

If you are really serious about your request, and you find an agency claiming one of the above exemptions, this side of going to court you may try contacting your Congressman or Senator. The exemptions are not authority to withhold information from Congress.

CHAPTER 4

Industrial Espionage

"The individual deals with the Government in a number of protected relationships which could be destroyed if the right to know were not modulated by principles of confidentiality and privacy."—ATTORNEY GENERAL RAMSEY CLARK

Contrary to what one might imagine, members of the news media are not the primary users of the Freedom of Information Act. Nor are public-interest groups, historians or researchers. Instead, the score cards kept by various agencies show businessmen and attorneys-at-law leading the pack.

Attorneys who practice before Federal regulatory agencies use the Act as the major instrument to penetrate the once watertight Government record rooms and files.

"FOI makes my job a hell of a lot easier," says one D.C. attorney. "In the old days I had to second guess Uncle at every juncture. Then even the scrap paper was classified. But today the agencies must carefully document all their meetings and rulings. Sometimes I can get what I need with a telephone call. The most I'll have to invest is a letter and a 13-cent stamp."

Because of such activity Federal agency attorneys are uneasy, frustrated and plagued by sneak attacks. "My cases are always being undermined," complains one general counsel. "Every time I come up with a peg to hang a case on, the opposition pulls a zinger on us via FOIA."

In Washington, D.C., a town so topheavy with law firms that it is not uncommon to find attorneys driving taxis, staffs of legal researchers specialize in Freedom of Information "fishing expeditions." This, in turn, makes it necessary for the agencies to expand many FOI offices in order to be able to handle the requests within the set time limitations. The cost to the taxpayer is literally incalculable. "It seems our own staffs are more help to the private sector in building its cases than to us practicing within the confines of Government. I can't send in a letter and get people hopping. I have trouble getting assistance with a direct order to my deputy," confides another in-house Government counsel.

Another attorney says that when a judge rules that a particular firm involved in litigation does not have to produce certain records, he can "try an end run and go in under FOIA at the agency which can yield the identical data."

Businessmen are having a heyday too. A past Food and Drug Administration Commissioner, Alexander M. Schmidt, said that 90 percent of the requests his agency receives are for purposes of "industrial espionage." At one time, the Pharmaceutical Manufacturers Association became so worried that "trade secrets" might leak out that it filed a lawsuit to protect its member companies. The suit was dropped because PMA, it was reported, felt that "the fears which prompted industry to file a suit may well not be realized."

Not everyone would agree with this. The trade secret: provision of the Act is a troublesome one with which FDA and other Federal agencies have had to struggle continuously. "The records we maintain are often laden with trade secret or confidential commercial information and, as the recipient of an enormous number of FOI requests— we expect some 25,000 this year (1977)—we are called upon daily to make disclosure decisions that involve potentially valuable business information," admits Dr. Donald Kennedy, the present Commissioner of the Food and Drug Administration.

Corporate executives do not like the idea that some public servant, secure for life in a non-competitive cubicle and suspended in a sea of stagnant mediocrity, might inadvertently expose their company to a competitor or lack the commercial sensitivity to know a possible trespass maneuver. "It's not too much comfort to know that an army of tired paper pushers is guarding a multimillion dollar formula," gripes one corporate vice-president.

And Dr. Kennedy admits, "Because of the complexity and variety of information in our files, and the possibility that the significance of certain information would escape the attention of nonprofessional employees, we must frequently use physicians, scientists and other professionals to perform these tasks."

Some agencies are making attempts at sensitizing their employees. "We are educating our personnel about these (FOI) procedures and, most importantly, sensitizing them to the problem of confidential business information," Michael A. James, Deputy General Counsel, Environmental Protection Agency, told Congressman Paul McCloskey, Jr., at October, 1977 hearings on the business record exemption of the Act.

MR. McCLOSKEY: "I am interested in how EPA sensitizes its employees—just as a practical question."

MR. JAMES: "A great deal of this kind of educating and sensitizing is done over the telephone and through meetings, as well as by memos."

MR. McCLOSKEY: "And, as good lawyers, after those phone calls, you generally follow up with a letter confirming that these things were said over the telephone; do you not?"

MR. JAMES: "Probably rather seldom."

The fear of Government disclosure is perhaps best exemplified by the following cases in point.

S. L. Terry, vice president, Public Responsibility and Consumer Affairs, Chrysler Corporation, in a letter to the Government Information and Individual Rights Subcommittee of the Committee on Government Operations, dated October 11, 1977.

"Chrysler Corporation provides information to the Federal Government in many capacities including that of taxpayer, employer, issuer of securities, government contractor and motor vehicle manufacturer. Reporting of much of such information is required by statute, regulation or order. However, Chrysler supplies a substantial amount of information to the Federal Government, not under threat of any sanction but purely because the Government has asked for it, has promised to keep it confidential, and Chrysler desires to be a good citizen.

". . . However, Chrysler is becoming increasingly concerned that these promises will be meaningless in the face of Freedom of Information Act requests. Grounds for such concern are based on published decisions of the courts, such as *Legal Aid Society of Alameda County v. Schultz*, 349 F Supp 771 (ND Cal '72), where the court said:

". . . administrative promises of confidentiality cannot extend the command of the Freedom of Information Act that only matters 'specifically exempted from disclosure by *statute*' are protected . . . it is now well settled that because of the specific command of 552 (c), discussed above, the courts have no discretion to refuse to order disclosure on equitable principles . . ."

"Furthermore, even if an FOIA exemption is available, providers of information such as Chrysler have absolutely no assurance that the Government will raise exemption as a shield against disclosure. By his letter of May 5, 1977 to "Heads of All Federal Departments and Agencies," Attorney General Griffin Bell advised that:

"The Government should not withhold documents unless it is important to the public interest to do so, even if there is some arguable legal basis for the withholding. In order to implement this view, the Justice Department will defend Freedom of Information Act suits only when disclosure is demonstrably harmful even if the documents technically fall within the exemptions in the Act."

"Thus, it appears the Government requests information on promises of confidentiality which it cannot keep and, even worse, has no intention of keeping."

James H. Hanes, vice president and general counsel, Dow Chemical Co., expressed similar concerns to Congressman Richardson Preyer of North Carolina.

"With growing U.S. trade deficits and, for example, with the obvious need for new and improved technology to solve both our short- and long-term energy needs, innovators must be rewarded for their contributions to the solution of these and other problems. We fear that, unless the technology which will solve our problems is protected against industrial espionage, there will be absolutely no incentive for private industry to generate such technology.

"A few years ago, the Dow Chemical Company was involved in negotiations with a foreign firm regarding the sale or exchange of Dow technology relating to a proprietary process for producing a commercial product. During the negotiations, Dow was required by a federal agency to submit certain information about this process to the agency. Two other U.S. producers of this product were also required to submit information about their processes to the same agency. A short while later, the foreign firm indicated to Dow that they were no longer interested in the process details which Dow had submitted to the agency. Upon investigating the matter with the agency, it was learned that the foreign firm had obtained from the agency under the Freedom of Information Act, copies of the information submitted by both Dow and the two other U.S. producers.

"From these facts, it is clear that the foreign firm was able to obtain at no cost some of three U.S. competitors' technology for which it otherwise would have had to furnish adequate consideration."

All of this activity has given birth to a small but ever-growing cottage industry in Washington, D.C.—document detective agencies. For a fee, these quick-moving and resourceful FOI service companies will hop, skip and jump all over the Federal Triangle digging out information for corporations trying to be one up on their competition.

For example, the FDA maintains a daily log, open to the general public, which lists those people making requests for information under the Freedom of Information Act. The log may show that Robbins has requested data on Hoffman-LaRoche. This snowballs when other firms duplicate the request to see just what it is that Robbins wants to know about Hoffman-LaRoche. You may even find Hoffman-LaRoche countering with a request to find out what it is Robbins is snooping into. The situation can become even more dramatic when the corporations hide behind operatives of FOI service companies for the requests.

One reported case involved the Upjohn Company. In a single communication it requested copies of 73 letters of inquiry submitted by others, along with copies of the data furnished by the FDA in response to 56 of those letters and 15 miscellaneous items including manuals, directories, and meeting minutes.

Preparing to sue a vaccine manufacturer, one attorney asked the FDA for "all documents or other information disclosable to use from FDA, NIH, DBS, HEW, the Department of Compliance and all other governmental agencies which may have helpful and useful information."

Sometimes it is possible to ferret out information on a mere thin thread of evidence. There was the case of a Washington State miller who got wind of the fact that an outside firm was going to construct a lumber mill in his area. He wanted to know if it was true. With only this information to go on, within a few hours a D.C. document detective dredged up the appropriate information without graft, snooping or any other trickery. The searcher just walked into the Environmental Protection Agency, which regulates lumber mills, and found that the EPA had on file an application to build a mill near his client.

The amount of information that is available and the ease with which it can be secured is on the rise. New Federal regulations are forcing private companies to put a great deal of never-before-released "inside" information on the public record.

Another target agency is the Securities and Exchange Commission. The SEC monitors approximately 12,000 public corporations, and maintains an enormous preserve of records which are of great value to investment hunters. Its library, open to the public, is becoming more and more important to corporations because of the vast storehouse of information it contains.

By keeping an eye on a competitor's SEC dossier, one can learn the financial stability of a corporation, future plans for expansion, stock purchases, etc. "There's no doubt that private attorneys and their clients are completely frightened of dealing with us," says SEC enforcement chief Stanley Sporkin. "They know the least dereliction potentially becomes a matter for public scrutiny even if an enforcement agency does not act."

In May of 1977 the SEC was forced to give up 28 cardboard boxes containing records amassed during its probe of illegal or questionable payments by nine U.S. firms. The SEC handed over the documents—reluctantly—in reply to requests filed by the news media under the FOIA.

One of the most dramatic cases revealed by these files involves the Remington Arms Company (a Du Pont subsidiary) which greased a customs agent, in an unidentified country, with an $18,000 bribe to make sure a larger import duty would not be levied on the firm. A pistol backed up the threat!

At one point the SEC actually told the firms it regulates that they must mark in advance what is to be confidential information supplied during an investigation. Otherwise, it said, the information may be made public once the case is closed.

"Every once and a while we will test the way the agencies are protecting the information we are forced to provide," a corporate counsel admits. "Going by way of an intermediary, we will slap an agency with a highly specific FOI request for proprietary information. If we get it, well, there's trouble in River City."

Indeed, it is very possible that all these FOI requests could well lead to an inadvertent disclosure of business information which should otherwise be kept classified. A wise man once said, "In confusion there is profit." This is exactly what those who pelt the agencies with FOI requests hope will happen.

The Federal Trade Commission faces a similar barrage of requests for information which might benefit parties subject to Commission jurisdictions. Here too the largest part of the FOI requests comes in from law firms and corporations.

"I remember when the FTC had an assortment of laws which wiped out investigative subpoenas. Everything over there was *sub rosa*," recalls another D.C. attorney. "There was no sure way for me to advise my clients how to handle subpoenas. The decisions and precedents were all secret. But today anyone can find them. They are open for public inspection."

The American Association of Advertising Agencies once asked the FTC for a staff study on the relationship of drug advertising to drug abuse. This, needless to say, saved the AAAA some big money.

Several insurance companies and lawyers requested an FTC staff memorandum discussing the Commission's jurisdiction over the insurance business.

Over at the Civil Aeronautics Board if a carrier loses a case before the Board, it can request all the backup material upon which the decision was made so that it may challenge the ruling in court.

Oil companies continually request information on their

competitors which has been compiled by the Department of Energy.

Freedom of Information is a mixed blessing for private industry, however. Not only are many companies able to invade and in turn be subject to invasion, but bureaucratic blunders can put them in danger without outside prompting.

AT&T president Charles L. Brown sent off an angry letter to Vice President Mondale in late August, 1977, concerning a study done for the White House Office of Telecommunications Policy on "the vulnerability of various commonly available electronic communications means to interception." The first two volumes of the $47,-000 study prepared by the MITRE Corporation were the common esoteric technical reports and of little interest to anyone outside of the field.

But Volume #3, which was smuggled out of the White House last summer, caused quite a rumbling. It is a how-to manual, using unclassified material in the first two volumes, and was written in such an elementary style that even the most amateurish of wire-tappers could use it with no tutoring.

Part one explains how to bug "a suburban residential telephone" in an "area similar to that found in Northern Virginia outside the Beltway." The steps include: "1. Visually trace drop wire to the distribution terminal. 2. Climb pole, open terminal enclosure and note color code of the (wire) pair in the distribution cable to which the drop wire is attached . . ."

Part two instructs one on the most efficient way to intercept a business's data communication to a computer terminal, "e.g. the business might have the computer handling all their accounting." Here, some of the steps include, "4. Dig a trench from building to branch feeder cable and dig up cable. 5. Install gas pressurization by-pass. Drill two small holes (say 24 inches apart) in cable sheath, being careful not to damage wire pairs and clamp by-pass to the two holes."

Part three shows how to tap calls from long distances. "The interceptor . . . knows the difficulties of penetrating . . . coaxial cable systems. He is aware of the high voltage hazards and the monitoring and alarm systems associated with the coaxial cables . . ." Therefore, one should bug the microwave relay as follows: "1. Locate microwave repeater sites for the route of interest either through physical observation or from FCC filings. 2. Acquire the use of a small farm along the route . . ." And so on.

Vice President Mondale has asked Frank Press, the Science Advisor to the President, to prevent official public disclosure of the volumes. He put the legal beagles at the White House, Justice, Management and Budget, OTP, and Defense to work on seeing if there is some way the more than one hundred FOI requests for the documents can be denied. Nevertheless, nothing is apt to stop the reproduction of the already bootlegged copies.

Not all information is sought to get one up on a rival in the marketplace. Many people seek corporate information for completely unselfish reasons.

Mr. Tony Mazzocchi of the Oil, Chemical and Atomic Workers International Union (OCAW) AFL-CIO charged that the "trade secrets" exemption of the FOI Act was being abused, causing serious health hazards to workers.

"Under OSHA regulations, an employer can declare any part of his manufacturing process to be a trade secret," he says. "Once the declaration is made, the inspector will abide by the wishes of the employer. Employees are not given an opportunity to challenge management's contention. This kind of carte blanche for employers could lead to arbitrary and capricious actions.

"For years, the industrial water wastes inventory was delayed because industry contended that trade secrets would be revealed if they had to describe the nature of the poisons being dumped into American rivers and streams," Mazzocchi points out. He further says that an employer can declare the toxic air contaminants inside a plant to be a trade secret. "The Labor Department will support him as the Office of Management and Budget supported the water polluters. Workers will never know what they are breathing until it's too late."

Information in such cases was also denied to the union under the "investigatory files" exemption of the FOI Act, according to Mazzocchi.

"Our inability to secure the type of information that is lifesaving information, really, in our opinion, is just contrary to the intent of the Freedom of Information Act, and the Department is hanging its hat for the most part on No. 7, investigatory files compiled for law enforcement purposes—holding that anything happening under the Occupational Health and Safety Act is for investigatory and law enforcement purposes, which means that we would be consistently denied information, the crucial information."

Sooner or later FOIA may, indeed, break this kind of information loose. However, since timeliness becomes of the utmost importance in such cases, when the information ultimately becomes available, sometimes it is really too late.

Thus, as the language of exemption (b) (7) of the Act has been interpreted, it makes it difficult, if not at times impossible, for workers in hazardous plants to be informed about specific health or safety problems that exist in an interim period while inspector's reports are slowly making their way through the bureaucracy toward eventual enforcement proceedings, fines, and corrective action. Obviously, this use of the Act is contrary to sound public policy in such situations where the lives of millions of American workers may be at stake. This case and others have prompted a reexamination of the language in this exemption. The only way such mistakes will be righted is by a constant public pressure via similar requests and appeals.

Here is yet another example of how citizens tried to use the Freedom of Information Act to obtain information which affects natural gas rate case decisions of the Federal Power Commission involving billions of dollars in higher gas rates for millions of consumers. The story of how the FPC withheld information is graphic, timely and illustrative of how business and Government can combine to use FOI exemptions against the citizenry.

Data on natural gas reserves, compiled by a committee of the American Gas Association and used by the FPC in making their rate increase determination in a southern Louisiana rate case, was withheld from consumer-oriented groups who sought to make an independent evaluation of the data. Stung by public and congressional criticism of their dependence on industry-furnished gas reserve studies, the Commission ordered a limited check of certain gas reserve data supplied by the AGA. The Commission, however, ordered that the data involved be kept confidential and withheld from the public. It was in this context that the Freedom of Information Act became an issue.

The FPC claimed secrecy under the Natural Gas Act and the Freedom of Information Act. The part used in the FOIA dealt with trade secrets and commercial or financial information obtained from a person and privileged or confidential . . . and (9) which concerns geological and geophysical information and data, including maps concerning wells.

The Federal Government plays an enormous role in the business world as a major purchaser of goods and services and as a regulator of industry. We are all aware of the large quantities of commercial information acquired by the Government. Much of this information involves the functions and operations of the Federal agencies and is releasable under the Freedom of Information Act.

However, Congress has always realized that some information supplied to the Government from private parties should not be released. This is to protect the rights of those who submit the information and to insure the necessary flow of data to the Government.

Submitters of information are always concerned that confidential information will be released to competitors, and that they will not be notified of the pending release in time to present arguments in favor of the confidential treatment of the documents. On the other hand, requesters of the information complain that too much is being withheld without adequate justification, and that the timeliness of release required by the FOIA is being ignored.

One must hope that the original intent of the law will balance out one day. But, for the time being, it appears that a free-for-all will continue in the war for information. And, it seems, both the Federal government and private industry are equally guilty of misusing the Act.

CHAPTER 5

Personal Dossiers

"No bureaucrat is going to admit he might have made a mistake."—CONGRESSMAN JOHN E. MOSES

We Americans have the right to participate in those processes which utilize personal information in reaching decisions that may affect our lives. No one will argue that the individual's right of privacy requires that personal information collected and held in government files under census collecting laws, income tax reporting laws, criminal investigations, and other activities, be protected from disclosure; nor can it be argued that the individual has no right to see personal dossiers and confirm that they are accurate, complete, up-to-date, and relevant to the purpose of the particular government agency.

One cannot assume that all the information contained in personal dossiers is accurate and/or relevant. An example of the kinds of information Uncle Sam salts away about a person is best illustrated by the cases of two citizens. The first requested his Army Intelligence file and was shocked at what he found. The file was put together in 1963 when the man was getting a security clearance.

"It said I owed 50 cents to my high school for not returning my locker key," he told a reporter. "That shows you the kind of stuff your high school keeps. It said that I dated two or three times per week, but that I was never intimate with my dates. How did they know? It also said I was financially irresponsible because I owed $5 for a jaywalking ticket to the city of Seattle. The scope of the trivia that goes into these things is absolutely mind-boggling."

Number two involves a young New Jersey co-ed, who, in preparation for a term paper, wrote for information to a political party that was included on the now-defunct Attorney General's list of subversive organizations. When FBI mail surveillance of the Young Socialist Alliance (an affiliation of the Socialist Workers Party) brought up the high school student's letter, FBI agents began snooping around her hometown—inquiring about her character, her father's credit line, and possible family police records. When the FBI agent discovered that the letter was merely part of a political-science project, the file was closed and the investigation ceased. However, apparently, FBI headquarters maintained an active file on her "subversive connection."

A U.S. district court judge in Newark ordered the FBI to destroy all the records it had compiled on the girl.

The Federal Government is a vast storehouse of information concerning individual citizens. For example:

If you have worked for a Federal agency or Government contractor or have been a member of any branch of the armed services, the Federal Government has a file on you.

If you have participated in any federally financed project, some agency probably has a record of it.

If you have been arrested by local, State or Federal authorities and your fingerprints were taken, the FBI maintains a record of the arrest.

If you have applied for a government subsidy for farming purposes, the Department of Agriculture is likely to have this information.

If you have received veterans' benefits, such as mortgage or education loans, employment opportunities, or medical services, the Veterans Administration has a file on you.

If you have applied for or received a student loan or grant certified by the Government, the Department of Health, Education and Welfare has recorded this information.

If you have applied for or been investigated for a security clearance for any reason, there is a good chance that the Department of Defense has a record of it.

If you have received medicare or social security benefits, the Department of Health, Education, and Welfare has a file on you.

In addition, Federal files on individuals include such items as:

Investigatory reports of the Federal Communications Commission concerning whether individuals holding Citizens Band and/or amateur radio licenses are violating operating rules.

Records of the Internal Revenue Service listing the names of individuals entitled to undeliverable refund checks.

Records compiled by the Department of State regarding the conduct of American citizens in foreign countries.

This is just a fraction of the information held on individual citizens. In fact, if you have ever engaged in any activity that you think might be of interest to the Federal Government, chances are very good that some Federal agency has a file on you.

Your freedom to the information contained in such files

is safeguarded under the Privacy Act of 1974 and it is under this Act that such information is made available.

THE PRIVACY ACT

The Privacy Act of 1974 is the culmination of many years of public and congressional debate and concern over the threat posed to individual privacy by the Federal Government's increasing acquisition of vast quantities of personal information on American citizens. IMPORTANT: *Unlike the FOIA—which applies to anyone making a request including foreign nationals as well as American citizens—the Privacy Act applies only to American citizens and aliens lawfully admitted for permanent residence.*

The underlying purpose of the Privacy Act is to give citizens more control over what information is collected by the Federal Government about them and how that information is used. The Act accomplishes this in five basic ways.

1. It requires agencies to publicly report the existence of all systems of records maintained on individuals.

2. It requires that the information contained in these record systems be accurate, complete, relevant, and up-to-date.

3. It provides procedures whereby individuals can inspect and correct inaccuracies in almost all Federal files about themselves.

4. It specifies that information about an individual gathered for one purpose not be used for another without the individual's consent.

5. It requires agencies to keep accurate accounting of the disclosure of records and, with certain exceptions, to make these disclosures available to the subject of the records.

In addition, the bill provides sanctions to enforce these provisions.

The Privacy Act applies only to personal records maintained by the executive branch of the Federal Government concerning individual citizens. It does not apply to records held by State and local governments or private organizations. The Federal agencies covered by the Act include executive departments and offices, military departments, government corporations, government controlled corporations, and independent regulatory agencies.

LOCATING YOUR RECORDS

If you think that a particular agency maintains records concerning you, you should write to the head of that agency or to the Privacy Act Officer. Agencies are required to inform you, at your request, whether they have files on you.

If you want to make a more thorough search to determine what records Federal departments may have on you, consult the compilation of Privacy Act notices published annually by the *Federal Register*. This multivolume work contains:

A. Descriptions of all Federal record systems.

B. Descriptions of the kinds of data covered by the systems.

C. Categories of individuals to whom the information pertains.

D. Procedures to follow at the different agencies.

E. Specification of the agency official to whom you should write.

This compilation is usually available in large reference, law, and university libraries. It can be purchased from the

Superintendent of Documents, Government Printing Office, Washington, D.C. 20402. The cost per volume runs around $6 to $12. But if you know which agency you are interested in, the Superintendent of Documents can help you identify the particular volume or volumes which contain the information you want. *Caveat Emptor!* The compilation is poorly indexed and, as a consequence, difficult to use. Therefore, you should examine the work before ordering it.

Don't worry if you cannot specify a particular record system which you think contains information on you; it is not necessary to provide the dossier.

THE REQUEST

You can make a request in writing, by telephone, or in person. The obvious advantage to writing is that it enables you to document the dates and contents of the request and the agency's replies. This could be helpful in future disputes. Be sure to keep all copies of such correspondence.

The letter should be addressed to the head of the agency which maintains the records you want or to the agency official in charge of the Privacy Act. Slug the request envelope with "Privacy Act Request/Do Not Delay." Give your telephone number in the letter to speed things up.

REMEMBER: *If your request arrives at the wrong office it will be forwarded and the agency will not begin its search until it reaches the proper office. This is particularly important in Privacy Act requests because unlike the Freedom of Information Act, which requires agencies to respond within 10 working days after receipt of a request, the Privacy Act imposes no time limits for agency responses.*

Most agencies require some proof of identity before they will release records. The CIA, for example, demands your date of birth, place of birth and a notorized statement of identity. If you are seeking access to a record which has something to do with a Government benefit, it could be helpful to provide your social security number. And some agencies may even request additional information such as a document containing your signature and/or photograph depending upon the nature and sensitivity of the material to be released.

WARNING! Anyone who "knowingly and willingly" requests or receives access to a record about an individual "under false pretenses" is subject to criminal penalties. This means that a person can be prosecuted for deliberately attempting to obtain someone else's record.

FEES

Under the Privacy Act, agencies are permitted to charge fees to cover the actual costs of copying records. However, they are not allowed to charge for the time spent in locating records or in preparing them for your inspection. Copying fees seem to run about 10¢ a page for standard size copies of 8 x 11 inches and 8 x 14 inches.

Since locating fees can be charged under the Freedom of Information Act, if you seek access to records under the Privacy Act which can be withheld under this act but are available under the FOIA, you could be charged search fees. In any case, if you ever feel that an agency's fees are beyond your means, you should ask for a reduction or waiver of the charges when making the initial request.

TIMETABLE

While there are no time limits for agency responses, the guidelines for implementing the Act's provisions recommended by the executive branch state that a request for records should be acknowledged within 10 working days of its receipt. Moreover, the acknowledgment should indicate whether or not access will be granted and, if so, when and where. The records themselves should be produced within 30 working days. And, if this is not possible, the agency should tell you the reason why and advise you when it anticipates to grant you access.

Most agencies will do their best to comply with these recommendations. Therefore, it is advisable to bear with some reasonable delay before taking further action. Two-thirds of the requests for information to the FBI alone fall under the Privacy Act. A Justice Department spokesperson estimates that in 1977 his agency received more than 80,000 requests for access to its records and perhaps as high as 68 percent counted as falling under the Privacy Act of 1974. Patience is the word.

APPEALS

Unlike the FOIA, the Privacy Act provides no standard procedure for appealing denials to release information. However, many agencies have their own regulations governing this. If your request is denied, the agency should advise you of its appeal procedure and tell you to whom to address your appeal. If this information is not provided, you should send a letter to the head of the agency. Include a copy of the rejection letter along with the copy of your original request and state your reason for wanting access, if you think it will help.

SAMPLE REQUEST

(Name and Address of Government Agency)

Washington, D.C. Zip Code

Re: Privacy Act Request

Dear (agency head or Privacy Act Officer):

Under the provisions of the Privacy Act of 1974, 5 U.S.C. 522a, I hereby request a copy of (or: access to) (describe the record or records you want and provide all the relevant information you have concerning them).

If there are any fees for copying the records I am requesting, please inform me before you fill the request. (Or: . . . please supply the records without informing me if the fees do not exceed $____.)

If all or any part of this request is denied, please cite the specific exemption(s) which you think justifies your refusal to release the information. Also, please inform me of your agency's appeal procedure.

In order to expedite consideration of my request, I am enclosing a copy of____(some document of identification). If you wish to discuss the matter, my telephone number is (Area Code + ____).

Thanking you in advance for your time and consideration, I am,

Sincerely,

REASONS WHY ACCESS MAY BE DENIED

Under the Privacy Act, certain systems of records can be exempted from disclosure. Agencies are required to publish annually in the *Federal Register* the existence and characteristics of all record systems, including those which have been exempted from access. However, just because records have been declared exempt does not mean they are beyond your reach, since agencies do not always use the exemptions they have claimed. Therefore, never hesitate to request any record you may desire. *The burden is on the agency to justify withholding the information from you.*

GENERAL EXEMPTIONS

The general exemptions apply only to the Central Intelligence Agency and criminal law enforcement agencies.

Exemption (j) (1): Files maintained by the CIA. This exemption permits the heads of the CIA to exclude certain systems of records within the Agency from many of the Act's requirements. The provisions from which the systems can be exempted are primarily those permitting individual access. Consequently, in most cases, you will probably not be allowed to inspect and correct records maintained by the CIA on you. But, again, there is no one saying you can't try.

Exemption (j) (2): Files maintained by Federal criminal law enforcement agencies. This exemption permits an agency to withhold records relating to police efforts to prevent control, or reduce crime or to apprehend criminals, and the activities of prosecutors, courts, correctional, probation, pardon or parole authorities, and which consist of (A) information compiled for the purpose of identifying individual criminal offenders and alleged offenders and consisting only of identifying data and notations of arrests, the nature and disposition of criminal charges, sentencing, confinement, release, and parole and probation status; (B) information compiled for the purpose of a criminal investigation, including reports of informants and investigators, and associated with an identifiable individual; or (C) reports identifiable to an individual compiled at any stage of the process of enforcement of the criminal laws from arrest or indictment through release from supervision.

By way of example, this exemption would permit the heads of such agencies as the FBI, the Drug Enforcement Administration, and the Immigration and Naturalization Service to exclude certain systems of records from the Act's requirements. As with the CIA, the allowed exemptions are primarily those permitting individual access. Remember, too, the Act explicitly states that records available under the FOIA must also be available under the Privacy Act. And under the FOIA, the CIA and FBI and other Federal agencies are required to release *all* non-exempt portions of their intelligence and investigatory files. Sometimes it is a good idea to cite both these acts when seeking information of an intelligence or investigatory nature.

SPECIFIC EXEMPTIONS

There are seven specific exemptions which apply to all agencies.

Exemption (k) (1): Classified documents concerning national defense and foreign policy.

This refers directly to the first exemption of the Freedom of Information Act (see page 28).

Exemption (k) (2): Investigatory material compiled for law enforcement purposes.

This applies to investigatory materials compiled for law enforcement purposes by agencies whose principal function is other than criminal enforcement. Included are such files as might be maintained by the Internal Revenue Service concerning, for example, taxpayers who are delinquent in filing Federal tax returns, records put together by the U.S. Customs Service on narcotic suspects, investigatory reports of the Federal Deposit Insurance Corporation concerning banking irregularities, and files maintained by the Securities Exchange Commission on individuals who are being investigated by the agency.

Again, such files cannot be withheld from you if they are used to deny you a benefit, right, or privilege to which you are entitled by law unless their disclosure would reveal the identity of a confidential source.

Exemption (k) (3): Secret Service intelligence files.

This exemption pertains to files held by the Secret Service that are necessary to insure the safety of the President of the United States and other individuals under Secret Service protection.

Exemption (k) (4): Files used solely for statistical purposes.

This covers such items as Internal Revenue Service files regarding the income of certain individuals used in computing national income averages, and records on births and deaths maintained by the Department of Health, Education, and Welfare for compiling U.S. vital statistics.

Exemption (k) (5): Investigatory material used in making decisions concerning Federal employment, military service, Federal contracts, and security clearances.

This exemption applies only to investigatory records which would reveal the identity of a confidential source. However, since it is not customary for agencies to grant pledges of confidentiality in collecting information concerning employment, Federal contracts, and security clearances, in most instances these records would be available.

If you ever applied to a Federal agency for employment, and subsequently either received or did not receive the job, this exemption should not hinder your efforts to see just what everyone interviewed had to say about you.

Exemption (k) (6): Testing or examination material used solely for employment purposes.

This exemption covers information which has been used to determine individual qualifications for appointment or promotion in the Federal service itself, information the disclosure of which might compromise the objectivity or fairness of the testing or examination process.

Exemption (k) (7): Evaluation material used in making decisions regarding promotions in the armed services.

This exemption is used only by the Armed Services. Moreover, due to the nature of military promotions where many individuals compete for the same assignment, it is often necessary to grant pledges of confidentiality in collecting information so that those queried about potential candidates will feel free to be candid in their assessments. Therefore, efficiency reports and other materials used in making decisions about military promotions may be hard to get. But always remember, when seeking information of an investigatory nature, it is a good idea to request it under both the Privacy Act and the Freedom of Information Act.

AMENDING YOUR RECORDS

The Privacy Act demands that all agencies maintain their personal files on individuals *accurate, complete, up-to-date,* and *relevant.* Therefore, if, after seeing your record, you wish to correct, delete, or add information to it, you should write to the agency official who released it to you, giving the reasons for the desired changes as well as any documentary evidence you might have to justify the changes.

If you have any doubts about anything you find in the file, you should not hesitate to challenge the information and force the agency to justify its retention in your file. Here's one thing you might look for: *The Privacy Act prohibits the maintenance of information concerning how an individual exercises his first amendment rights* unless (1) the maintenance is authorized by statute or the individual to whom it pertains, or (2) unless it is pertinent to and within the scope of an authorized law enforcement activity.

In most instances you would be on pretty solid ground in challenging any information in your file describing your religious and political beliefs, activities, and associations, unless you personally have voluntarily given this information to the agency.

The Act requires agencies to acknowledge in writing all requests for amending records within 10 working days of their receipt. Also, you must be advised what action will be taken on the requested amendments. The law says that agencies must complete such action on all such requests within 30 working days of their receipt.

SAMPLE REQUEST TO AMEND RECORDS

(Name and Address of Government Agency)
Washington, D.C. Zip Code

Re: Privacy Act Request to Amend Records

Dear (agency head or Privacy Act Officer):

By letter dated _____, I requested access to (use the same description as in your request letter).

In reviewing the information forwarded to me, I found that it was (inaccurate) (incomplete) (outdated) (not relevant to the purpose of your agency).

Therefore, pursuant to the Privacy Act of 1974, 5 U.S.C. 552a, I hereby request that you amend my record in the following manner: (Describe errors, new information, irrelevance, etc.)

In accordance with the Act, I look forward to an acknowledgment of this request within 10 working days of its receipt. If you wish to discuss this matter, my telephone number is (Area Code _____).

Thanking you in advance for your time and consideration, I am,

Sincerely,

Appeal Procedure for Agency Refusal to Amend Records

Here again the system is set up for an appeal procedure. If an agency refuses to amend the records, you must be advised the reasons for refusal as well as the appeal procedures available to you.

A decision on your appeal must be rendered within 30 working days from the date of its receipt. In unusual circumstances, such as the need to obtain information from retired records or another agency, an additional 30 days may be granted.

If the agency denies your appeal and still refuses to make the changes you request, you have the right to file a brief statement giving your reasons for disputing the record. This statement of disagreement then automatically becomes part of the record and *must* be forwarded to all past and future recipients of your file. The agency is also permitted to place in the file its side of the story. This, too, becomes part of the permanent file and is forwarded along with your statement of disagreement.

If your appeal is denied or if the agency fails to act upon it within the specified time, you can take the case to court.

Extra Rights Afforded Under the Privacy Act

1. Agencies must obtain your written permission prior to disclosing to other persons or agencies information concerning you, unless such disclosures are specifically authorized under the Act.

2. You are entitled to know to whom information about you has been sent. Agencies must maintain accurate accounting of all disclosures.

3. This information must be kept on file for at least 5 years or until the record disclosed is destroyed, whichever is longer.

With the exception of law enforcement agencies, a list of all recipients of information concerning you MUST be made available to you upon request. Therefore, if you further want to know who is seeing your files, drop a line to the Privacy Officer at the agency in question and ask for the list.

4. The Privacy Act places a moratorium upon any new uses of your social security number by Federal, State, and local government agencies after January 1, 1975. THIS IS THE ONLY PROVISION IN THE ACT WHICH APPLIES TO STATE AND LOCAL AS WELL AS FEDERAL AGENCIES.

This provision does not apply to the private sector! Any private organization can request your social security number.

CHAPTER 6

The Bureaucratic Blister

"It is not the function of our Government to keep the citizen from falling into error; it is the function of the citizen to keep the Government from falling into error."—ROBERT HOUGHWOUT JACKSON

"Most agencies would scrap it if they could," insists a staffer on one of the two subcommittees charged with jurisdiction over the Freedom of Information Act.

"It's not that the Federal bureaucrats are against the public's right to know, it's just that the Act makes waves, waves make work and work can produce mistakes, which seems to be the one thing bureaucrats cannot admit to making," the staffer continued. "FOI has made most bureaucrats 'gun shy.' "

"Getting information from the Executive is a day-to-day struggle. The confrontation is constant," says Dante B. Fascell, a Florida Congressman. "I was involved many years ago in a Department of Defense investigation on behalf of a congressional committee. DOD just shut the doors and would not let us see anything. The Comptroller General, who was helping us with this investigation, was denied access to all the documents dealing with the subject matter."

Congressman Fascell contends that open government would help eliminate the skepticism, the distrust and the frustration the people harbor. "There is the image of the backroom and the smoke-filled room where everyone is pulling strings, and the guy on the end of the string with his head in the noose is the average taxpayer."

"We should not accept national security claims or any other reasons that are given as a rationale for not having the American public understand that the Government is giving mere lip service to the notion that we can conduct an open society," states Congressman Michael Harrington of Massachusetts.

When Congressman Paul N. McCloskey, Jr. asked Donald Elisburg, Assistant Secretary for Employment Standards, Department of Labor, how many people his department has engaged in complying with Freedom of Information requests, the response was: "Too many, Congressman."

Elisburg's attitude seems emblematic of most bureaucrats concerning the cost and burden of responding to FOIA requests.

Dr. Donald Kennedy, Commissioner, Food and Drug Administration, echoed these sentiments. He contends, "Obviously, the time required to review records . . . is obviously time that is not spent on the substantive work of the Agency."

Perhaps the impact of FOI Act requests is nowhere better highlighted than over at the Environmental Protection Agency. Michael A. James, deputy general counsel, reports that for fiscal year 1976 (excluding the transition quarter), the EPA reported 3,352 requests in Washington and each regional office. Of these, 1,817 were from corporations, 398 were from law firms, 473 were from individuals, 253 were from State and local governments, 200 were from public interest groups and unions, 132 were from universities, 48 were from the media, and 31 were from congressional committees and Federal agencies. When he asked the EPA Freedom of Information for an up-date covering July 1, 1976 to June 30, 1977, it revealed that EPA headquarters received 917 requests from corporations, 202 from law firms, 124 from individuals, 77 from public interest groups, 55 from State and local governments, 48 from universities, 36 from the media, and 10 from Congress and Federal agencies.

He further states that in calendar year 1976, EPA initially denied 168 out of 4,113 requests received. Denials can also be time-consuming since they must usually be reviewed by a chain of officials before they are signed, a process that can take, on the average, 12 working days.

It was once reported that the House Committee on Government Operations felt FOIA would cost the Federal government no more than $100,000 per year to administrate.

The Defense Department alone expends more than $6 million on it annually. The Federal Bureau of Investigation, a source in the FOI office estimates, will spend more than $4.5 million on FOIA and Privacy Act requests in 1978. The figures for the Treasury Department, Health, Education, and Welfare, and the Central Intelligence Agency are all well into the millions of dollars too.

The actual cost to the taxpayer for Freedom of Information and Privacy Act requests is unknown. Accurate statistics do not exist anywhere.

"The Library of Congress does an analysis for the Senate but there is much underreporting," says another Capitol Hill staff assistant. "One-third of the departments and agencies give us figures—others don't. It seems to be a catch-as-catch-can situation."

The Federal agencies are so overwhelmed with paperwork concerning the Act that Freedom of Information offices had to be opened and staffed at more cost to the taxpayer.

According to Assistant Secretary Elisburg, the number of person hours used by the Office of Federal Contract Compliance Programs for the administration of the requests filed under exemption (b) (4) *alone* of the FOIA for the period September 30, 1976, thru September 30, 1977, was 830. Person hours used for legal interpretation and processing lawsuits was 5,000.

In 1976, the Food and Drug Administration received almost 22,000 requests under FOIA and made only 309 denials. When asked for a rough ball park figure on how many of the 22,000 requests would have been granted even if they were not under FOI, Stuart Pape, office of the general counsel, answered: "It is almost an impossible question to give a guess on. You can go back historically to see the way we treated requests for information before the FOI Act came around. It was almost as if we had a rubber stamp that said "No." I think that we would readily concede that the passing of the Act was a great impetus at our agency in changing our policies.

"We went from a situation in which about 10 percent of our records were disclosed before the Act to a situation where now we estimate about 90 percent of the categories of records we have are disclosed."

One year the National Science Foundation received over 100 requests for information under the FOI Act from the same individual. The editor of a newsletter sent in an average of one request every two and a half working days, it was reported.

A CIA spokesperson says that "we'll never be totally up-to-date." A glance at the CIA FOIA request log shows you why. Here's a sample partial listing of what people have requested information about:

UFOs
The "Forever Family"
East Bay Women for Peace
A deceased brother
Where's What
Hypnosis
Union Nacional de Trabajadores de Puerto Rico
Marilyn Monroe
Amelia Earhart
UFOs
A deceased father
The role of missionaries and clergy in espionage
Where's What
UFOs
The death of Amelia Earhart
Dialogue Magazine
The Pacifica Foundation
Air America
Ali Sabry
The Atlantic City Christian Association
Syracuse University
Stavros Niarchos
Lehigh-Pocono Committee of Concern
The death of Amelia Earhart
Where's What
Antoine Gizenga
Brainwashing

The Freedom Center
Chicago Red Square
Airlie House and Conference Center
MKULTRA
UFOs
Dr. Mengele's whereabouts
The Los Angeles Free Clinic
The National Committee Against
    Repressive Legislation
Gran Oriente Nacional de Puerto Rico
UFOs
Where's What
Black Muslims
KOPOK-438
Franz Fanon
UFOs
Rev. Sun Myung Moon
The SLA
The Punta Aloe Corporation
Lee Harvey Oswald
A deceased husband
The U.S. March for Victory
Guerrilla troop movements in Mozambique and
    Guinea-Bissau
Jayne Mansfield
"Operation Unicorn"
Slovak National Uprising
WXUR-AM/FM
UFOs
Aristotle Onassis
Names of journalists working as agents for the CIA

General oversight into the administration of the Freedom of Information Act has been exercised by the Foreign

Operations and Government Subcommittee and the Senate Subcommittee on Administrative Practice and Procedure since the Act took effect on July 4th, 1967.

To the further dismay of many bureaucrats, the House subcommittee has provided informal assistance service in hundreds of cases involving the Act that have been referred by Members of Congress and their staffs or called to the subcommittee's attention by newsmen, radio-television broadcasters, researchers, attorneys, historians and scholars, and by individual citizens. It has also provided information about the Act and informal suggestions involving the procedural handling of Freedom of Information cases.

Peter R. Schuck, of the Center for the Study of Responsive Law, described his experience with the Agriculture Department as a "delay-until-the-information-becomes-stale" routine. He was trying to obtain information on meat inspection plants in Missouri under the Wholesome Meat Act of 1967.

Mr. William A. Dobrovir, a Washington, D.C., attorney, who has handled numerous freedom of information cases, says: "The first problem is the intransigence of Government officials. Basically, they believe that the public's business is their business, and not the business of the public."

Perhaps U.S. District Court Judge William B. Jones summed it up best when he said that various government agencies "don't like the Freedom of Information Act."

CHAPTER 7

Case Histories

"Every day, at lower levels of Government, Federal agencies have regrettably undertaken coverups which have also undermined the confidence of the American people in their Government."—U.S. SENATOR WALTER F. MONDALE

Freedom of Information requests and cases abound throughout the Federal bureaucracy. Did you know that it was under the Act that the FBI was forced to open its files on the assassinations of President John F. Kennedy, Robert Kennedy and the Reverend Martin Luther King, Jr.? Dossiers on Ezra Pound, Alger Hiss and the Rosenbergs also surfaced via FOIA. The disclosure that the Nixon White House instigated Internal Revenue Service investigations of social action groups on the left and in the black community was caused by FOIA requests. The alarming news of FBI counter-intelligence activities against "radical" organizations was pried loose with lawsuits under the Act. All this and much more is the result of concerned citizens exercising their rights to knowledge of the governments' activities and demanding accountability.

75

The new book, *Legend: The Secret World of Lee Harvey Oswald*, is the result of 2½ years of work by editors and researchers at *Reader's Digest* who found much of their material in FBI and CIA files released under the Freedom of Information Act.

But such research, albeit legitimate, is not always easy. The American Civil Liberties Union once studied the FBI's response to requests for historical information from scholars over a two-year period. The ACLU concluded that the FBI's historical records disclosure rate was a dismal failure. In case after case, significant historical research was curtailed by administrative restrictions which seemed arbitrary and unnecessary and heavy costs of time and money were imposed upon the persons seeking access. Here's a case in point.

Professor Sander Gilman, chairman of the Department of German Literature at Cornell University, was preparing a biography of the German playwright and poet, Bertolt Brecht. The FBI's first response said that it had "approximately 1,000 pages" in its files on Brecht and that Gilman would have to "submit letters from Brecht's heirs granting their approval" to his research. Then the FBI would provide him with the materials at a "processing" cost of $160.

One month later, Professor Gilman sent the Bureau a deposit and a letter to him from Brecht's only son, dated a week earlier, which stated that the son had "no objection to your use of the FBI files on my father." Two months later the FBI provided Gilman with 30 heavily deleted pages from its Brecht files as the "final disposition" of his request. It refused to produce the bulk of the requested files on the ground that Gilman had not provided the Bureau with written authorization from the heirs of each of the hundreds of persons—many of them public figures, such as Thomas Mann, author—whose names appear in the files. Included within the 30 pages—3 percent of the entire file, for which Gilman paid $40—were 8-10 magazine and newspaper clippings on Brecht's well-publicized travels throughout the United States.

On the following pages I've written up some well-known and some not-so-well-known cases involving FOIA requests. They represent a cross section of the many thousands of requests Washington receives. They may assist you in a quest to establish precedents or just to have an idea of what is going on at the different fronts of action. All are true and accurate accounts and, by their very nature, are now themselves part of the public record.

The CIA's Top-Secret "Boo-Boo"

In January, 1977, the world was shocked by the news that Israel had produced nuclear weapons as early as 1974. The source of this unnerving information? A document, which had been previously stamped "Secret. No Foreign Disclosure," entitled "Prospects for Further Proliferation of Nuclear Weapons," a resume of a top-secret special CIA intelligence report, was released in error under the Freedom of Information Act.

S. Jacob Scherr, a lawyer for the National Resources Defense Council, Inc., an environmental association, had requested the paper from our newest Federal agency, the Department of Energy. As the document carried a top-secret classification, DOE automatically sent if off to the CIA in Langley, Virginia, asking that it make the decision whether any portions of the summary could be given sunlight under the Freedom of Information Act.

Reportedly the document was examined closely by not

one but several CIA departments prior to the deletion of two paragraphs and release of the remainder.

Herbert E. Hetu, a CIA spokesman, said the document's release was a "mistake." "Maybe there was a glitch in the system," said a spokesman for the Nuclear Regulatory Commission, as he tried to fathom why Joseph Hendrie, the NRC's chairman, and Clifford Smith, director of its office of nuclear materials safety and safeguards, had never seen copies of the top-secret summary.

The news broke during the difficult and highly delicate Middle East negotiations. "This thing could raise hell with the Middle East peace efforts," one U.S. senator who asked not to be named told a reporter. "If the Israelis have weapons the other side will want to even it up."

The document, written just after the 1974 Indian A-bomb explosion, also cautioned that Taiwan, Argentina, and South Africa may also have A-bombs soon. The document also states that some U.S. intelligence officers felt that "Japan's leaders will conclude that they must have nuclear weapons if they are to achieve their national objectives in the developing Asian power balance."

Pandora's Box may be opened even wider, since this document is sure to concentrate more interest on stories that 206 pounds of highly enriched uranium, which was reportedly unexplainably "lost" at a private nuclear fuel manufacturing complex at Apollo, Pennsylvania, in the mid-1960s, may have been secretly re-routed to Israel.

In the face of this controversy, Stansfield Turner, CIA Director, told *Time*, in an exclusive interview, "I'm just so proud of what we have contributed in the past nine months to the public debate on major issues. . . . All these (Soviet studies) have given the taxpayer a greater return on his investment in intelligence. I intend to keep on with this program. I will be criticized sometimes for supporting the Administration's policy and sometimes for not supporting it. I'm doing neither. I'm giving the information we have."

ILLEGALLY OPERATED POLICE RADAR

Often just the mention of the Freedom of Information Act will open Federal government files. This was the case with Rex Power, a Maryland resident who was tired of receiving speeding citations for infractions of the 55-mph limit when he knew he was well within the posted speeds.

Power made the assumption that if he wasn't speeding, perhaps the problem was with the radar equipment being used by the police.

The files on radar (called *radiopositioning equipment* by the FCC) devices are maintained by the Chief Engineer, Laboratory Division, Federal Communications Commission, in Laurel, Maryland. It is here that the FCC type-accepts all the gear. Type-acceptance is the testing of the equipment for frequency stability, performance under various weather conditions, such as prolonged exposure to temperatures and humidities, and the effect on operation when the position of the equipment and surrounding objects is changed, to name but a few of the tests.

The only attempt to thwart Power's entry was denying him the use of copying facilities even if he was willing to pay for the service. He was not frustrated by this in the least. The same afternoon, he arrived at the Laurel complex with his own desk top copier and began to read the files. After Power had read and copied over half of the files, the FCC officer in charge denied him access to all other files unless he were to come in under an official FOIA request. But it was too late. Power had not only found the information he sought, but he also found out two other facts, perhaps more important than what he had originally come to obtain.

Firstly, he found that, in at least one instance, a manufacturer had sold radiopositioning equipment to a State police force prior to the FCC's seal of type-acceptance. How had the FCC found out? Letters exist from the president of one major manufacturer to the FCC alerting the Agency to the fact that one of his competitors was soliciting and accepting orders on equipment that had not yet passed the FCC review.

Secondly, he found out that before a police agency is permitted to legally operate radiopositioning equipment the Federal Communications Commission must license it. Since the radar transmitter, like thousands of other devices, radiates energy which uses the radio-frequency spectrum, it comes under the regulatory umbrella of the FCC. While the licenses are free and quite easy to obtain, Power was surprised to find that most of the U.S. police departments were (and probably still are!) operating without licenses—therefore, illegally.

Mr. Power, a free lance writer, took this information, and more, and wrote the most comprehensive book on the subject of radar as an effective traffic control device. Entitled, *How to Beat Police Radar . . . and Do It Legally,* the book immediately caused panic in police departments throughout the nation. After the Associated Press and United Press International ran major news stories on his findings, the citizenry started asking questions. In Tucson, Arizona, for example, all the police radiopositioning equipment was pulled from the streets immediately. It was revealed that this equipment had been unlicensed—although used to raise over $250,000 in fines—for over four years. At this writing the controversy is just starting and will surely be in the courts for years to come.

By the way, it was later reported that Mr. Power did, indeed, beat his speeding rap with the information he found on file.

HELP FOR THE HANDICAPPED

Mr. John Seigenthaler, editor of the Nashville *Tennessean,* suspected that a blind homeowner might have been swindled on the basis of an FHA appraisal of his property. The homeowner and, later, the newspaper asked the Department of Housing and Urban Development for a copy of the FHA appraisal, but they were both refused. The Nashville *Tennessean* took the case to court. The judge set a hearing in two weeks, but the Government lawyers demanded the full 60 days permitted under the Federal Rules of Civil Procedure to answer the newspaper's request for access to a public record.

After the hearing, the court ordered the Government agency to make public a copy of the FHA appraisal, but the copy which was ultimately turned over to the newspaper was totally and completely illegible.

Once more, the newspaper went to court and the judge ordered the Government to produce a legible copy of the FHA appraisal report. The district court did agree with the Government's contention that it could censor the FHA appraisal report, deleting the name of the appraiser.

The newspaper took that issue to the circuit court of appeals, and once more, over the opposition and delaying tactics of the Government agency, won a court order granting access to a legible public record—including the identity of the FHA appraiser.

SOME SIMPLE QUESTIONS TO THE IRS

The delays and frustrations faced by citizens asking Federal agencies for information are nowhere more apparent than in the attempt by a Seattle, Washington, couple to get some data from the Internal Revenue Service. Among the documents requested by Philip and Susan Long were those with simple statistical information showing how the IRS carries out its tax collecting duties. They also requested the blank forms which IRS agents fill out as a basis for an annual activities report. After repeated trips to IRS headquarters in Washington, D.C., and some to a number of regional and field operations, the Longs did get some of the public records they had requested. But the balance of the material was made available by IRS only after the Longs filed suit under the Freedom of Information Act.

Because of the continued prodding by the Longs, IRS prepared a dossier on the couple, listing every letter sent by them and every interview with IRS officials. When faced with the Longs' request for the blank IRS forms, Donald Virdin, Chief of the IRS Disclosure Staff, convened 18 top officials to discuss the disclosure problem. The panel of top officials decided the Longs could not have the blank forms because there were too many of them.

As a result of handling the Longs' request for public records, the Treasury Department discovered some IRS documents in its public library which, according to Virdin, should not have been made public. What were these classified documents? They were merely quarterly reports on the audit work of IRS, but upon Virdin's recommendation the reports were taken out of the public library, no longer to be disclosed.

The most appalling part of this case is that Mr. Virdin's staff of disclosure experts also prepared a digest of the IRS experience for public records under the Freedom of Information Act. And when another taxpayer requested to read the digest, he was refused! The document had been classified "for national office official internal use only." Needless to say, soon thereafter the digest was made public with the secrecy label removed.

"CATCH-22" AT THE AGRICULTURE DEPARTMENT

The Freedom of Information Act requires Government agencies to make available "identifiable" public records, but the Attorney General's Memorandum explaining the law warns that the identification requirement should not be used as a method of withholding records. Yet some agencies try to make identification requirements so strict that they must often be taken to court to force co-operation (*Bristol-Myers Co. v. Federal Trade Commission,* 283 F Supp. 745; *Wellford v. Hardin,* 315 F. Supp. 768).

Harrison Wellford of the Center for the Study of Responsive Law once asked the Department of Agriculture for research on the safety of handling certain pesticides. His request was refused because the Government records he sought were not clearly identified.

Wellford then asked for the indexes the Department maintained so the specific files could be identified, but he was told that the indexes were interagency memoranda and would not be made available.

"So, it was a Catch-22 situation," Wellford testified. "We were told our request was not specific, and we were not given access to the indexes which would have allowed us to make our request specific."

Wellford took his case to court and won access to the information. He went back to the Agriculture Department, looked at the indexes, and found that the information he sought was kept in individual folders called jackets. He was told that the jackets also contained confidential company information and that the confidential information had not been separated from the technical information he sought.

"We requested this information two years before and there was plenty of time to reorganize their filing systems so they would not have this commingling problem. . . . The final straw was when USDA stated that if the information were made available, it would cost $91,840 to prepare the registration files for public viewing. At that point we decided to try to find other means to get the information." Hence the court case.

The "Renting" of the Pentagon

Even before the Columbia Broadcasting System produced its controversial exposé of the Defense Department propaganda machine—a program entitled "The Selling of the Pentagon"—the Freedom of Information Act was twisted almost out of shape by Defense Department officials trying to hide the facts about the "renting" of the Pentagon. Repeated delays and insistence on bureaucratic formalities were almost successful in hiding from the public how much money the Department collects in concession payments from private companies which have stores in the Pentagon concourse.

Roy McGhee, a reporter for United Press International, asked for the financial details on the leasing of store space in the bowels of the Pentagon where thousands of employees pass daily on their way to bus stops inside the building. He found, after repeated telephone calls, that the Defense Department collected almost $1 million in proceeds from private companies doing business on the Pentagon concourse. He reported that about half of this income was turned over to the Treasury and the rest was contributed to a Defense Department "Concessions Committee," which used about $250,000 of the fund to finance social clubs, dinner dances and tennis tournaments for Pentagon employees.

But he said he could not obtain an exact accounting of the use of such funds, nor could he discover how much each private company was paying the Pentagon to lease space in the concourse and sell wares to thousands of captive customers. He asked the Department's public information office and he asked the Department's general counsel how much each private company was paying to lease space in the public building; but the information was refused.

Since McGhee's company did not file a lawsuit to get the information, he just wrote a news story based upon the information he could find, reporting the refusal to disclose the income from leasing of the Pentagon concourse space, and the University of Missouri Freedom of Information Center took up the battle from there. The Center telephoned to try to get the information and then put a formal request in writing, threatening to go to court under the Freedom of Information Act if the information was refused. The Defense Concessions Committee agreed to make public the contracts entered into with private companies leasing space in the Pentagon, but only if a records search charge of $3.45 an hour was paid for a four hour search job.

As the Defense Departments Concessions Committee was responsible for only 16 contracts, all filed in the committee's office, the FOI Center pointed out that four hours for searching the files to find the contracts seemed an unnecessary waste of time. In response, more than one year after McGhee first began his investigation of the "renting" of the Pentagon, the Defense Department Concessions Committee finally agreed to make the information of the contracts available to anyone who came into the committee's Pentagon office—if given one day advance notice!

THE SKY'S A-GOING TO FALL

The fiery plunge of a Soviet Cosmos satellite into the atmosphere over Canada in January, 1978, triggered concern worldwide about the more than 4,000 satellites and "cosmic junk" still orbiting the earth. People started asking questions about how much of this we may expect to fall and when and where.

One such person was a student in Scranton, Pennsylvania, Cole Richards. Upon reading about the malfunctioning satellite, he immediately contacted the Public Information Officer at the North American Air Defense Command (NORAD) to find out some history. The NORAD officer suggested that he contact both the Smithsonian Astrophysical Observatory and NASA at the Goddard Space Flight Center. These two organizations told Richards that in addition to the 4,000 satellites, more than 4,881 decayed objects—space junk—was also revolving over us. "On the average something decays each day of the year," said one official.

The problem came when Richards asked for information on all cases known to the United States Government. NASA and the Smithsonian Institution insisted that the Air Force kept such records and the Air Force said such data was classified.

After several phone calls to the Pentagon, he directed a FOI request to FTD/DADF, Foreign Technology Division, Wright Patterson AFB, OH 45433, in which he asked for any reports listing space junk investigations which involved the U.S.A.F.

What he received was the official "Space Object Fragment Summary." The document lists some 47 startling examples of "space junk" that did not disintegrate and/or hit bodies of water.

Did you know that in September, 1962, a cylindrical metal piece (diameter 15 centimeters, weight 21 pounds) hit a street intersection in Manitowoc, Wisconsin? It was identified as part of Soviet Sputnik IV, launched May 15, 1960.

In May, 1964, a charred piece of electronic equipment (weight 175 pounds) was found near La Fria, Venezuela. It was later identified as part of a DOD satellite launched April 27, 1964, which decayed May 26, 1964.

In October, 1966, Wisconsin was the target again. Near Tomahawk, a titanium spherical pressure vessel (diameter 14.7 inches, weight 30 pounds) hit and was identified merely as Soviet in origin.

The most frightening report came in August, 1970, when five oblong pieces of steel (2 to 2.5 feet long, average weight 150 pounds) and one flat steel plate (4 by 4 feet, weight 640 pounds) lacerated the earth's crust in Kansas, Texas and Oklahoma. They were parts from Soviet Cosmos 316, launched December 23, 1969; they decayed August 28, 1970.

The report further points out that in September, 1974, May, 1975, and January, 1976, areas around Lowell, Ohio; Winter Haven, Florida; and Marietta, Ohio, respectively, were hit by falling debris.

With the "Space Object Fragment Summary" in hand, Richards wrote back to FTD/DADF for more information on the Soviet Sputnik IV that fell in Manitowoc, Wisconsin. The letter he received back said, "FTD has reviewed the files and cannot find any information on the Soviet Sputnik IV that fell on a street intersection in Manitowoc, WI, in September 1962." At this writing

Richards is assuming the answer is a denial to his request and has an FOI appeal under way. It is apparent that someone at Wright-Patterson is not aware that the "Space Object Fragment Summary" is out!

A PRISONER ENGAGES THE FOIA

Douglas Wayne Thompson has served some 15 years behind bars in Missouri federal prisons. In his spare time he taught himself about law, freedom of information, and became extremely interested in working for penal reform. Therefore, he felt knowledgeable and confident enough on August 7, 1975, to slap a suit against the Missouri Council on Criminal Justice so that it would have to release the records of all its correctional programs and all Law Enforcement Assistance Administration grant fund expenditures made by the Missouri Division of Corrections.

On February 20, 1976, the Missouri Council on Criminal Justice filed a motion to dismiss the suit, which Thompson countered five days later. Then nothing happened until a March, 1976, pre-trial meeting at which time the defendants suggested that the cost of reproducing the 15 filing cabinets of paperwork was too much to expect. Thompson quickly targeted his request on only the audit reports on all grant expenditures, in particular those for the Missouri Board of Parole.

To placate Thompson, the defendants sent him between March and September of 1976 a total of 10 audit reports. Thompson said that by that time the parole board had received over 100 LEAA grants. The 10 audit reports covered only 20 programs.

At the next pre-trial conference, the defendants said that they could only surrender 10 audit reports. Thompson refused to drop his suit and decided to stonewall it.

A U.S. magistrate took on the case on January 14, 1977.

On February 15th the magistrate ordered Thompson to show cause why the suit should not be thrown out of court as frivolous. Thompson, a serious student of the Freedom of Information Act, showed the magistrate where the law he (the magistrate) was citing related to provisions of the 1966 FOIA that were no longer relevant in light of subsequent amendments to the law.

On April 28th at another pre-trial conference, it was agreed that within 30 days the Missouri assistant attorney general would visit Thompson at the Missouri Training Center for Men at Moberly and hand over the requested data. The official never showed up!

After three months of waiting for this visitor, Thompson received a letter from the assistant attorney general apologizing for the delay and asking Thompson to send him the names, addresses and telephone numbers of any witnesses that he might have asked to drop in at the offices of the law council and obtain the reports. Thompson never provided this information and to date has heard nothing else.

Thompson was reported to have said, "All they have been interested in is getting rid of the suit by trying to trick me in any number of ways, which only makes me more determined than ever to win and get these audit reports. In fact, this kind of funny business only makes me think for certain there is something in the reports."

DECEASED BLACK INTELLECTUALS

In April of 1977 the Federal Bureau of Investigation was ordered to compile an index of historical documents which had hitherto been withheld from Ben Waknin, who wanted information on the careers of black intellectuals from 1914-1929.

The FBI tried to claim exemption under the basis of law-enforcement and inter- or intra-agency memoranda. A deputy attorney general informed the FBI that it could only withhold these documents on the grounds of national security.

A district court judge ruled that his decision was binding and said, "it beggars credulity to believe that any document sought by plaintiff, concerning black intellectuals of a long bygone era, could impinge upon our national defense or foreign policy." Then while referring to the manner in which Waknin's freedom of information request was handled, the judge said this case "places in stark and dismaying contrast the bold pronouncements of the Freedom of Information Act . . . with the bureaucratic confusion and spirit of grudging acquiescence with which that legislation has been greeted by some of our Federal agencies."

PUSHED AROUND BY U.S. CUSTOMS

After several years overseas with a major U.S. multi-national corporation, Louis Williams was asked home to New York City to discuss re-assignment with his superiors. However, to his surprise, what had in the past always been a routine entry at John F. Kennedy International Airport became a nightmare. For no apparent reason, when he arrived at the luggage inspection belt area, he was rushed off to a nearby interrogation room by agents of the U.S. Customs Service.

According to Williams he was made to leave his suitcases unattended where they could have been stolen and then he was subjected to "degrading and abusive" questioning concerning a minor disagreement over several gifts he had purchased overseas. He charged that one of the agents went so far as to take his driver's license and automobile registration.

The next day Williams shot a letter off to the Customs Commissioner in Washington, D.C. in which he described his ordeal and demanded a full investigation and that all the records of inquiry be sent to him.

U.S. Customs officials advised him that it was "not our policy" to provide such documents. Williams refused to give up. In another letter to the Customs Commissioner he gave him an up-date then said that "I believe your office has behaved in an arbitrary and capricious manner."

The U.S. Customs Service did not provide Williams with the records he requested until about one month after he filed suit in U.S. District Court. But when the records were turned over to him they were "subject to certain deletions." Among the deletions were the names of the U.S. Customs agents involved. The exemption claimed was that such disclosure would "endanger the life or physical safety of law enforcement personnel."

The judge who was handling Williams' suit found it hard to justify the exemption claim. In a subsequent ruling he held that "the circumstances surrounding the withholding of this information raise questions as to whether agency personnel acted arbitrarily or capriciously with respect to the withholding of the requested information."

The judge then ordered a U.S. marshal to serve a copy of his findings on the Chairman of the Civil Service Commission "so that he might promptly initiate a proceeding to determine whether disciplinary action is warranted against those primarily responsible for the illegal withholding. . . ."

The Federal government came back several days later with a request for an elaborate bid for a modification of the judge's order. Uncle Sam claimed that the Customs officials had used the "utmost diligence" after receiving Williams' appeal and held "many inter-office meetings and exchanges of memoranda on the merits of the case. . . ."

Williams said the government's case was full of holes. The judge denied the government petition for re-consideration.

CONTROVERSY AT U.S. MILITARY ACADEMIES

In recent years cadet honor codes and many cadets at U.S. military academies have been tarnished by various scandals. Americans are concerned and, in at least one instance, took one of the service academies to court under a Freedom of Information lawsuit. Here's what happened.

The instance involved an Air Force Academy graduate who, in preparation for a law review article on military academy honor codes, requested case summaries from his Colorado Springs alma mater. The Air Force refused to release the documents, so law review editors instituted suit under the Freedom of Information Act, ultimately pursuing their case to the U.S. Supreme Court.

Case summaries are usually distributed to faculty and administrators and even wind up posted on approximately 40 bulletin boards on academy grounds. Summaries involving cadets found not guilty (or otherwise permitted to return to their squadrons in good standing) are circulated with the names deleted; those involving guilty verdicts are circulated without such deletions, but only after the cadets in question have resigned from the academy.

Quick to admit that it was an agency covered by the Freedom of Information Act, the Air Force Academy cited two exemptions in the Act as support for not releasing the summaries: Exemption 2, authorizing withholding of documents "related solely to the internal personnel rules and practices of an agency"; and Exemption 6, pertaining to "personnel and medical files and similar files the disclosure of which would constitute a clearly unwarranted invasion of personal privacy."

Justice William Brennan, writing for the majority, shot the Air Force's case from the sky. He dismissed each of these exemptions in turn. It was determined that Exemption 2 was designed to cover only minor and trivial matters, not those in which the public might be legitimately interested. And, he added, the administration of honor codes at public military academies is of more than minor public interest.

"The implication for the general public of the Academy's administration of discipline is obvious, particularly so in light of the unique role of the military. . . .

"Since the purpose of the Honor and Ethics Code administered and enforced at the Air Force Academy is to ingrain the ethical reflexes basic to these responsibilities in future Air Force officers, and to select out those candidates apparently unlikely to serve these standards, it follows that the nature of this instruction—and its adequacy or inadequacy—is significantly related to the substantive public role of the Air Force and its academy. Indeed, the public's stake in the operation of the codes as they affect the training of future Air Force officers and their military careers is underscored by the Agency's own proclamations of the importance of cadet-administered codes to the academy's educational training programs. . . .

"In sum, we think that, at least where the situation is not where disclosure may risk circumvention of agency regulation, Exemption 2 is not applicable to matters subject to such a genuine and significant public interest . . ."

The majority also held that Exemption 6 did not completely insulate the summaries from disclosure.

As the same public interest would apply to codes of ethics for similar government employees, a similar procedure would presumably be ordered if any Federal agency sought to shield such matters from public inquiry.

Lower court judges may now determine such cases.

APPENDIX A

FULL TEXT OF FREEDOM OF INFORMATION ACT, AS AMENDED IN 1974 BY PUBLIC LAW 93-502

§ 552.   Public information; agency rules, opinions, orders, records, and proceedings

(a) Each agency shall make available to the public information as follows:

(1) Each agency shall separately state and currently publish in the Federal Register for the guidance of the public—

(A) descriptions of its central and field organization and the established places at which, the employees (and in the case of a uniformed service, the members) from whom, and the methods whereby, the public may obtain information, make submittals or requests, or obtain decisions;

(B) statements of the general course and method by which its functions are channeled and determined, including the nature and requirements of all formal and informal procedures available;

(C) rules of procedure, descriptions of forms available or the places at which forms may be obtained, and instructions as to the scope and contents of all papers, reports, or examinations;

(D) substantive rules of general applicability adopted as authorized by law, and statements of general policy or interpretations of general applicability formulated and adopted by the agency; and

(E) each amendment, revision, or repeal of the foregoing.

Except to the extent that a person has actual and timely notice of the terms thereof, a person may not in any manner be required to resort to, or be adversely affected by, a matter required to be published in the Federal Register and not so published. For the purpose of this paragraph, matter reasonably available to the class of persons affected thereby is deemed published in the Federal Register when incorporated by reference therein with the approval of the Director of the Federal Register.

(2) Each agency, in accordance with published rules, shall make available for public inspection and copying—

(A) final opinions, including concurring and dissenting opinions, as well as orders, made in the adjudication of cases;

(B) those statements of policy and interpretations which have been adopted by the agency and are not published in the Federal Register; and

(C) administrative staff manuals and instructions to staff that affect a member of the public;

unless the materials are promptly published and copies offered for sale. To the extent required to prevent a clearly unwarranted invasion of personal privacy, an agency may delete identifying details when it makes available or publishes an opinion, statement of policy, interpretation, or staff manual or instruction. However, in each case the justification for the deletion shall be explained fully in writing. Each agency shall also maintain and make available for public inspection and copying current indexes providing identifying information for the public as to any matter issued, adopted, or promulgated after July 4, 1967, and required by this paragraph to be made available or published. Each agency shall promptly publish, quarterly or more frequently, and distribute (by sale or otherwise) copies of each index or supplement thereto unless it determines by order published in the Federal Register that the publication would be unnecessary and impracticable, in which case the agency shall nonetheless provide copies of such index on request at a cost not to exceed the direct cost of duplication. A final order, opinion, statement of policy, interpretation, or staff manual or instruction that affects a member of the public may be relied on, used, or cited as precedent by an agency against a party other than an agency only if—

(i) it has been indexed and either made available or published as provided by this paragraph; or

(ii) the party has actual and timely notice of the terms thereof.

(3) Except with respect to the records made available under paragraphs (1) and (2) of this subsection, each agency, upon any request for records which (A) reasonably describes such records and (B) is made in accordance with published rules stating the time, place, fees (if any), and procedures to be followed, shall make the records promptly available to any person.

(4)(A) In order to carry out the provisions of this section, each agency shall promulgate regulations, pursuant to notice and receipt of public comment, specifying a uniform schedule of fees applicable to all constituent units of such agency. Such fees shall be limited to reasonable standard charges for document search and duplication and provide for recovery of only the direct costs of such search and duplication. Documents shall be furnished without charge or at a reduced charge where the agency determines that waiver or reduction of the fee is in the public interest because furnishing the information can be considered as primarily benefiting the general public.

(B) On complaint, the district court of the United States in the district in which the complainant resides, or has his principal place of business, or in which the agency records are situated, or in the District of Columbia, has jurisdiction to enjoin the agency from withholding agency records and to order the production of any agency records improperly withheld from the complainant. In such a case the court shall determine the matter de novo, and may examine the contents of such agency records in camera to determine whether such records or any part thereof shall be withheld under any of the exemptions set forth in subsection (b) of this section, and the burden is on the agency to sustain its action.

(C) Notwithstanding any other provision of law, the defendant shall serve an answer or otherwise plead to any complaint made under this subsection within thirty days after service upon the defendant of the pleading in which such complaint is made, unless the court otherwise directs for good cause shown.

(D) Except as to cases the court considers of greater importance, proceedings before the district court, as authorized by this subsection, and appeals therefrom, take precedence on the docket over all cases and shall be assigned for hearing and trial or for argument at the earliest practicable date and expedited in every way.

(E) The court may assess against the United States reasonable attorney fees and other litigation costs reasonably incurred in any case under this section in which the complainant has substantially prevailed.

(F) Whenever the court orders the production of any agency records improperly withheld from the complainant and assesses against the United States reasonable attorney fees and other litigation costs, and the court additionally issues a written finding that the circumstances surrounding the withholding raise questions whether agency personnel acted arbitrarily or capriciously with respect to the withholding, the Civil Service Commission shall promptly initiate a proceeding to determine whether disciplinary action is warranted against the officer or employee who was primarily responsible for the withholding. The Commission, after investigation and consideration of the evidence submitted, shall submit its findings and recommendations to the administrative authority of the agency concerned and shall send copies of the findings and recommendations to the officer or employee or his representative. The administrative authority shall take the corrective action that the Commission recommends.

(G) In the event of noncompliance with the order of the court, the district court may punish for contempt the responsible employee, and in the case of a uniformed service, the responsible member.

(5) Each agency having more than one member shall maintain and make available for public inspection a record of the final votes of each member in every agency proceeding.

(6)(A) Each agency, upon any request for records made under paragraph (1), (2), or (3) of this subsection, shall—

(i) determine within ten days (excepting Saturdays, Sundays, and legal public holidays) after the receipt of any such request whether to comply with such request and shall immediately notify the person making such request of such determination and the reasons therefor, and of the right of such person to appeal to the head of the agency any adverse determination; and

(ii) make a determination with respect to any appeal within twenty days (excepting Saturdays, Sundays, and legal public holidays) after the receipt of such appeal. If on appeal the denial of the request for records is in whole or in part upheld, the agency shall notify the person making such request of the provisions for judicial review of that determination under paragraph (4) of this subsection.

(B) In unusual circumstances as specified in this subparagraph, the time limits prescribed in either clause (i) or clause (ii) of subparagraph (A) may be extended by written notice to the person making such request setting forth the reasons for such extension and the date on which a determination is expected to be dispatched. No such notice shall specify a date that would result in an extension for more than ten working days. As used in this subparagraph, "unusual circumstances" means, but only to the extent reasonably necessary to the proper processing of the particular request—

(i)   the need to search for and collect the requested records from field facilities or other establishments that are separate from the office processing the request;

(ii)   the need to search for, collect, and appropriately examine a voluminous amount of separate and distinct records which are demanded in a single request; or

(iii)   the need for consultation, which shall be conducted with all practicable speed, with another agency having a substantial interest in the determination of the request or among two or more components of the agency having substantial subject-matter interest therein.

(C) Any person making a request to any agency for records under paragraph (1), (2), or (3) of this subsection shall be deemed to have exhausted his administrative remedies with respect to such request if the agency fails to comply with the applicable time limit provisions of this paragraph. If the Government can show exceptional circumstances exist and that the agency is exercising due diligence in responding to the request, the court may retain jurisdiction and allow the agency additional time to complete its review of the records. Upon any determination by an agency to comply with a request for records, the records shall be made promptly available to such person making such request. Any notification of denial of any request for records under this subsection shall set forth the names and titles or positions of each person responsible for the denial of such request.

(b) This section does not apply to matters that are—

(1) (A) specifically authorized under criteria established by an Executive order to be kept secret in the interest of national defense or foreign policy and (B) are in fact properly classified pursuant to such Executive order;

(2) related solely to the internal personnel rules and practices of an agency;

(3) specifically exempted from disclosure by statute;

(4) trade secrets and commercial or financial information obtained from a person and privileged or confidential;

(5) inter-agency or intra-agency memorandums or letters which would not be available by law to a party other than an agency in litigation with the agency;

(6) personnel and medical files and similar files the disclosure of which would constitute a clearly unwarranted invasion of personal privacy;

(7) investigatory records compiled for law enforcement purposes, but only to the extent that the production of such records would (A) interfere with enforcement proceedings, (B) deprive a person of a right to a fair trial or an impartial adjudication, (C) constitute an unwarranted invasion of personal privacy, (D) disclose the identity of a confidential source and, in the case of a record compiled by a criminal law enforcement authority in the course of a criminal investigation, or by an agency conducting a lawful national security intelligence investigation, confidential information furnished only by the confidential source, (E) disclose investigative techniques and procedures, or (F) endanger the life or physical safety of law enforcement personnel;

(8) contained in or related to examination, operating, or condition reports prepared by, on behalf of, or for the use of an agency responsible for the regulation or supervision of financial institutions; or

(9) geological and geophysical information and data, including maps, concerning wells.

Any reasonably segregable portion of a record shall be provided to any person requesting such record after deletion of the portions which are exempt under this subsection.

(c) This section does not authorize withholding of information or limit the availability of records to the public, except as specifically stated in this section. This section is not authority to withhold information from Congress.

(d) On or before March 1 of each calendar year, each agency shall submit a report covering the preceding calendar year to the Speaker of the House of Representatives and President of the Senate for referral to the appropriate committees of the Congress. The report shall include—

(1) the number of determinations made by such agency not to comply with requests for records made to such agency under subsection (a) and the reasons for each such determination;

(2) the number of appeals made by persons under subsection (a)(6), the result of such appeals, and the reason for the action upon each appeal that results in a denial of information;

(3) the names and titles or positions of each person responsible for the denial of records requested under this section, and the number of instances of participation for each;

(4) the results of each proceeding conducted pursuant to subsection (a)(4)(F), including a report of the disciplinary action taken against the officer or employee who was primarily responsible for improperly withholding records or an explanation of why disciplinary action was not taken;

(5) a copy of every rule made by such agency regarding this section;

(6) a copy of the fee schedule and the total amount of fees collected by the agency for making records available under this section; and

(7) such other information as indicates efforts to administer fully this section.

The Attorney General shall submit an annual report on or before March 1 of each calendar year which shall include for the prior calendar year a listing of the number of cases arising under this section, the exemption involved in each case, the disposition of such case, and the cost, fees, and penalties assessed under subsections (a)(4)(E), (F), and (G). Such report shall also include a description of the efforts undertaken by the Department of Justice to encourage agency compliance with this section.

(e) For purposes of this section, the term "agency" as defined in section 551(1) of this title includes any executive department, military department, Government corporation, Government controlled corporation, or other establishment in the executive branch of the Government (including the Executive Office of the President), or any independent regulatory agency.

APPENDIX B

PUBLIC LAW 93-579:
THE PRIVACY ACT OF 1974

Be it enacted by the Senate and House of Representatives of the United States of America in Congress assembled, That this Act may be cited as the "Privacy Act of 1974."

Sec.2.

(a)　The Congress finds that—
　　(1)　the privacy of an individual is directly affected by the collection, maintenance, use, and dissemination of personal information by Federal agencies;
　　(2)　the increasing use of computers and sophisticated information technology, while essential to the efficient operations of the Government, has greatly magnified the harm to individual privacy that can occur from any collection, maintenance, use, or dissemination of personal information;
　　(3)　the opportunities for an individual to secure employment, insurance, and credit, and his right to due process, and other legal protections are endangered by the misuse of certain information systems;
　　(4)　the right to privacy is a personal and fundamental

right protected by the Constitution of the United States; and

(5) in order to protect the privacy of individuals identified in information systems maintained by Federal agencies, it is necessary and proper for the Congress to regulate the collection, maintenance, use, and dissemination of information by such agencies.

(b) The purpose of this Act is to provide certain safeguards for an individual against an invasion of personal privacy by requiring Federal agencies, except as otherwise provided by law, to—

(1) permit an individual to determine what records pertaining to him are collected, maintained, used, or disseminated by such agencies;

(2) permit an individual to prevent records pertaining to him obtained by such agencies for a particular purpose from being used or made available for another purpose without his consent;

(3) permit an individual to gain access to information pertaining to him in Federal agency records, to have a copy made of all or any portion thereof, and to correct or amend such records;

(4) collect, maintain, use, or disseminate any record of identifiable personal information in a manner that assures that such action is for a necessary and lawful purpose, that the information is current and accurate for its intended use, and that adequate safeguards are provided to prevent misuse of such information;

(5) permit exemptions from the requirements with respect to records provided in this Act only in those cases where there is an important public policy need for such exemption as has been determined by specific statutory authority; and

(6) be subject to civil suit for any damages which occur as a result of willful or intentional action which violates any individual's rights under this Act.

Sec.3.

Title 5, United States Code, is amended by adding after section 552 the following new section:

"552a. Records maintained on individuals

"(a) DEFINITIONS.—For purposes of this section—

"(1) the term 'agency' means agency as defined in section 552(e) of this title;

"(2) the term 'individual' means a citizen of the United States or an alien lawfully admitted for permanent residence;

"(3) the term 'maintain' includes maintain, collect, use, or disseminate;

"(4) the term 'record' means any item, collection, or grouping of information about an individual that is maintained by an agency, including, but not limited to, his education, financial transactions, medical history, and criminal or employment history and that contains his name, or the identifying number, symbol, or other identifying particular assigned to the individual, such as a finger or voice print or a photograph;

"(5) the term 'system of records' means a group of any records under the control of any agency from which information is retrieved by the name of the individual or by some identifying number, symbol, or other identifying particular assigned to the individual;

"(6) the term 'statistical record' means a record in a system of records maintained for statistical research or reporting purposes only and not used in whole or in part in making any determination about an identifiable individual, except as provided by section 8 of title 13; and

"(7)   the term 'routine use' means, with respect to the disclosure of a record, the use of such record for a purpose which is compatible with the purpose for which it was collected.

"(b)   CONDITIONS OF DISCLOSURE.—No agency shall disclose any record which is contained in a system of records by any means of communication to any person, or to another agency, except pursuant to a written request by, or with the prior consent of, the individual to whom the record pertains, unless disclosure of the record would be—

"(1)   to those officers and employees of the agency which maintains the record who have a need for the record in the performance of their duties;

"(2)   required under section 552 of this title;

"(3)   for a routine use as defined in subsection (a)(7) of this section and described under subsection (e)(4)(D) of this section;

"(4)   to the Bureau of the Census for purposes of planning or carrying out a census of survey or related activity pursuant to the provisions of title 13;

"(5)   to a recipient who has provided the agency with advance adequate written assurance that the record will be used solely as a statistical research or reporting record, and the record is to be transferred in a form that is not individually identifiable;

"(6)   to the National Archives of the United States as a record which has sufficient historical or other value to warrant its continued preservation by the United States Government, or for evaluation by the Administrator of General Services or his designee to determine whether the record has such value;

"(7)   to another agency or to an instrumentality of any governmental jurisdiction within or under the control of the United States for a civil or criminal law enforcement activity if the activity is authorized by law, and if the head of the agency or instrumentality has made a written request to the agency which maintains the record specifying the particular portion desired and the law enforcement activity for which the record is sought;

"(8) to a person pursuant to a showing of compelling circumstances affecting the health or safety of an individual if upon such disclosure notification is transmitted to the last known address of such individual;

"(9) to either House of Congress, or, to the extent of matter within its jurisdiction, any committee or subcommittee thereof, any joint committee of Congress or subcommittee of any such joint committee;

"(10) to the Comptroller General, or any of his authorized representatives, in the course of the performance of the duties of the General Accounting Office; or

"(11) pursuant to the order of a court of competent jurisdiction.

"(c) ACCOUNTING OF CERTAIN DISCLOSURES.—
Each agency, with respect to each system of records under its control, shall—

"(1) except for disclosures made under subsections (b)(1) or (b)(2) of this section, keep an accurate accounting of—

"(A) the date, nature, and purpose of each disclosure of a record to any person or to another agency made under subsection (b) of this section; and

"(B) the name and address of the person or agency to whom the disclosure is made;

"(2) retain the accounting made under paragraph (1) of this subsection for at least five years or the life of the record, whichever is longer, after the disclosure for which the accounting is made;

"(3)   except for disclosures made under subsection (b)(7) of this section, make the accounting made under paragraph (1) of this subsection available to the individual named in the record at his request; and

"(4)   inform any person or other agency about any correction or notation of dispute made by the agency in accordance with subsection (d) of this section of any record that has been disclosed to the person or agency if an accounting of the disclosure was made.

"(d)   ACCESS TO RECORDS.—Each agency that maintains a system of records shall—

"(1)   upon request by any individual to gain access to his record or to any information pertaining to him which is contained in the system, permit him and upon his request, a person of his own choosing to accompany him, to review the record and have a copy made of all or any portion thereof in a form comprehensible to him, except that the agency may require the individual to furnish a written statement authorizing discussion of that individual's record in the accompanying person's presence;

"(2)   permit the individual to request amendment of a record pertaining to him and—

"(A)   not later than 10 days (excluding Saturdays, Sundays, and legal public holidays) after the date of receipt of such request, acknowledge in writing such receipt; and

"(B)   promptly, either—

"(i)   make any correction of any portion thereof which the individual believes is not accurate, relevant, timely, or complete; or

"(ii)   inform the individual of its refusal to amend the record in accordance with his request, the reason for the refusal, the procedures established by the agency for the individual to request a review of that refusal by the head of the agency or an officer designated by the head of the agency, and the name and business address of that official;

"(3) permit the individual who disagrees with the refusal of the agency to amend his record to request a review of such refusal, and not later than 30 days (excluding Saturdays, Sundays, and legal public holidays) from the date on which the individual requests such review, complete such review and make a final determination unless, for good cause shown, the head of the agency extends such 30-day period; and if, after his review, the reviewing official also refuses to amend the record in accordance with the request, permit the individual to file with the agency a concise statement setting forth the reasons for his disagreement with the refusal of the agency, and notify the individual of the provisions for judicial review of the reviewing official's determination under subsection $(g)(1)(A)$ of this section;

"(4) in any disclosure, containing information about which the individual has filed a statement of disagreement, occurring after the filing of the statement under paragraph (3) of this subsection, clearly note any portion of the record which is disputed and provide copies of the statement and, if the agency deems it appropriate, copies of a concise statement of the reasons of the agency for not making the amendments requested, to persons or other agencies to whom the disputed record has been disclosed; and

"(5) nothing in this section shall allow an individual access to any information compiled in reasonable anticipation of a civil action or proceeding.

"(e) AGENCY REQUIREMENTS.—Each agency that maintains a system of records shall—

"(1) maintain in its records only such information about an individual as is relevant and necessary to accomplish a purpose of the agency required to be accomplished by statute or by executive order of the President;

"(2) collect information to the greatest extent practicable directly from the subject individual when the information may result in adverse determinations about an individual's rights, benefits, and privileges under Federal programs;

"(3) inform each individual whom it asks to supply information, on the form which it uses to collect the information or on a separate form that can be retained by the individual—

"(A) the authority (whether granted by statute, or by executive order of the President) which authorizes the solicitation of the information and whether disclosure of such information is mandatory or voluntary;

"(B) the principal purpose or purposes for which the information is intended to be used;

"(C) the routine uses which may be made of the information, as published pursuant to paragraph (4)(D) of this subsection; and

"(D) the effects on him, if any, of not providing all or any part of the requested information;

"(4) subject to the provisions of paragraph (11) of this subsection, publish in the *Federal Register* at least annually a notice of the existence and character of the system of records, which notice shall include—

"(A) the name and location of the system;

"(B)   the categories of individuals on whom records are maintained in the system;

"(C)   the categories of records maintained in the system;

"(D)   each routine use of the records contained in the system, including the categories of users and the purpose of such use;

"(E)   the policies and practices of the agency regarding storage, retrievability, access controls, retention, and disposal of the records;

"(F)   the title and business address of the agency official who is responsible for the system of records;

"(G)   the agency procedures whereby an individual can be notified at his request if the system of records contains a record pertaining to him;

"(H)   the agency procedures whereby an individual can be notified at his request how he can gain access to any record pertaining to him contained in the system of records, and how he can contest its content; and

"(I)   the categories of sources of records in the system;

"(5)   maintain all records which are used by the agency in making any determination about any individual with such accuracy, relevance, timeliness, and completeness as is reasonably necessary to assure fairness to the individual in the determination;

"(6)   prior to disseminating any record about an individual to any person other than an agency, unless the dissemination is made pursuant to subsection (b)(2) of this section, make reasonable efforts to assure that such records are accurate, complete, timely, and relevant for agency purposes;

"(7)   maintain no record describing how any individual

exercises rights guaranteed by the First Amendment unless expressly authorized by statute or by the individual about whom the record is maintained or unless pertinent to and within the scope of an authorized law enforcement activity;

"(8)   make reasonable efforts to serve notice on an individual when any record on such individual is made available to any person under compulsory legal process when such process becomes a matter of public record;

"(9)   establish rules of conduct for persons involved in the design, development, operation, or maintenance of any system of records, or in maintaining any record, and instruct each such person with respect to such rules and the requirements of this section, including any other rules and procedures adopted pursuant to this section and the penalties for noncompliance;

"(10)   establish appropriate administrative, technical, and physical safeguards to insure the security and confidentiality of records and to protect against any anticipated threats or hazards to their security or integrity which could result in substantial harm, embarrassment, inconvenience, or unfairness to any individual on whom information is maintained; and

"(11)   at least 30 days prior to publication of information under paragraph (4)(D) of this subsection, publish in the *Federal Register* notice of any new use or intended use of the information in the system, and provide an opportunity for interested persons to submit written data, views, or arguments to the agency.

"(f)   AGENCY RULES.—In order to carry out the provisions of this section, each agency that maintains a system of records shall promulgate rules, in accordance with the requirements (including general notice) of section 553 of this title, which shall—

"(1) establish procedures whereby an individual can be notified in response to his request if any system of records named by the individual contains a record pertaining to him;

"(2) define reasonable times, places, and requirements for identifying an individual who requests his record or information pertaining to him before the agency shall make the record or information available to the individual;

"(3) establish procedures for the disclosure to an individual upon his request of his record or information pertaining to him, including special procedure, if deemed necessary, for the disclosure to an individual of medical records, including psychological records, pertaining to him;

"(4) establish procedures for reviewing a request from an individual concerning the amendment of any record or information pertaining to the individual, for making a determination on the request, for an appeal within the agency of an initial adverse agency determination, and for whatever additional means may be necessary for each individual to be able to exercise fully his rights under this section; and

"(5) establish fees to be charged, if any, to any individual for making copies of his record, excluding the cost of any search for and review of the record.

The Office of the Federal Register shall annually compile and publish the rules promulgated under this subsection and agency notices published under subsection (e)(4) of this section in a form available to the public at low cost.

"(g) —

    "(1) CIVIL REMEDIES.—Whenever any agency

        "(A) makes a determination under subsection (d)(3) of this section not to amend an individual's record in accordance with his request, or fails to make such review in conformity with that subsection;

"(B)   refuses to comply with an individual request under subsection (d)(1) of this section;

"(C)   fails to maintain any record concerning any individual with such accuracy, relevance, timeliness, and completeness as is necessary to assure fairness in any determination relating to the qualifications, character, rights, or opportunities of, or benefits to the individual that may be made on the basis of such record, and consequently a determination is made which is adverse to the individual; or

"(D)   fails to comply with any other provision of this section, or any rule promulgated thereunder, in such a way as to have an adverse effect on an individual,

the individual may bring a civil action against the agency, and the district courts of the United States shall have jurisdiction in the matters under the provisions of this subsection.

"(2) —

"(A)   In any suit brought under the provisions of subsection (g)(1)(A) of this section, the court may order the agency to amend the individual's record in accordance with his request or in such other way as the court may direct. In such a case the court shall determine the matter *de novo*.

"(B)   The court may assess against the United States reasonable attorney fees and other litigation costs reasonably incurred in any case under this paragraph in which the complainant has substantially prevailed.

"(3) —

"(A) In any suit brought under the provisions of subsection (g)(1)(B) of this section, the court may enjoin the agency from withholding the records and order the production to the complainant of any agency records improperly withheld from him. In such a case the court shall determine the matter *de novo,* and may examine the contents of any agency records *in camera* to determine whether the records or any portion thereof may be withheld under any of the exemptions set forth in subsection (k) of this section, and the burden is on the agency to sustain its action.

"(B) The court may assess against the United States reasonable attorney fees and other litigation costs reasonably incurred in any case under this paragraph in which the complainant has substantially prevailed.

"(4) In any suit brought under the provisions of subsection (g)(1)(C) or (D) of this section in which the court determines that the agency acted in a manner which was intentional or willful, the United States shall be liable to the individual in an amount equal to the sum of—

"(A) actual damages sustained by the individual as a result of the refusal or failure, but in no case shall a person entitled to recovery receive less than the sum of $1,000; and

"(B) the costs of the action together with reasonable attorney fees as determined by the court.

"(5) An action to enforce any liability created under this section may be brought in the district court of the United States in the district in which the complainant resides, or has his principal place of business, or in which the agency records are situated, or in the District of Columbia, without regard to the amount in controversy, within two years from the date on which the cause of action arises, except that where any agency has materially and willfully misrepresented any information required under this section to be disclosed to an individual and the information so misrepresented is material to establishment of liability of the agency to the individual under this section, the action may be brought at any time within two years after discovery by the individual of the misrepresentation. Nothing in this section shall be construed to authorize any civil action by reason of any injury sustained as the result of a disclosure of a record prior to the effective date of this section.

"(h) RIGHTS OF LEGAL GUARDIANS.—For the purposes of this section, the parent of any minor, or the legal guardian of any individual who has been declared to be incompetent due to physical or mental incapacity or age by a court of competent jurisdiction, may act on behalf of the individual.

"(i) —

"(1) CRIMINAL PENALTIES.—Any officer or employee of an agency, who by virtue of his employment or official position, has possession of, or access to, agency records which contain individually identifiable information the disclosure of which is prohibited by this section or by rules or regulations established thereunder, and who knowing that disclosure of the specific material is so prohibited, willfully discloses the material in any manner to any person or agency not entitled to receive it, shall be guilty of a misdemeanor and fined not more than $5,000.

"(2) Any officer or employee of any agency who willfully maintains a system of records without meeting the notice requirements of subsection (e)(4) of this section shall be guilty of a misdemeanor and fined not more than $5,000.

"(3) Any person who knowingly and willfully requests or obtains any record concerning an individual from an agency under false pretenses be guilty of a misdemeanor and fined not more than $5,000.

"(j) GENERAL EXEMPTIONS.—The head of any agency may promulgate rules, in accordance with the requirements (including general notice) of sections 553(b)(1), (2), and (3), (c), and (e) of this title, to exempt any system of records within the agency from any part of this section except subsections (b), (c)(1) and (2), (e)(4)(A) through (F), (e)(6), (7), (9), (10), and (11), and (i) if the system of records is—

"(1) maintained by the Central Intelligence Agency; or

"(2) maintained by an agency or component thereof which performs as its principal function any activity pertaining to the enforcement of criminal laws, including police efforts to prevent, control, or reduce crime or to apprehend criminals, and the activities of prosecutors, courts, correctional, probation, pardon, or parole authorities, and which consists of (A) information compiled for the purpose of identifying individual criminal offenders and alleged offenders and consisting only of identifying data and notations of arrests, the nature and disposition of criminal charges, sentencing, confinement, release, and parole and probation status; (B) information compiled for the purpose of a criminal investigation, including reports of informants and investigators, and associated with an identifiable individual; or (C) reports identifiable to an individual compiled at any stage of the process of enforce-

ment of criminal laws from arrest or indictment
through release from supervision.

At the time rules are adopted under this subsection, the
agency shall include in the statement required under section 553(c) of this title, the reasons why the system of records is to be exempted from a provision of this section.

"(k) SPECIFIC EXEMPTIONS.—The head of any agency
may promulgate rules, in accordance with the requirements (including general notice) of sections 553(b)(1), (2),
and (3), (c), and (e) of this title, to exempt any system of
records within the agency from subsections (c)(3), (d),
(e)(1), (e)(4)(G), (H), and (I) and (f) of this section if the
system of records is—

"(1) subject to the provisions of section 552(b)(1) of this
title;

"(2) investigatory material compiled for law enforcement purposes, other than material within the
scope of subsection (j)(2) of this section: *Provided,
however,* that if any individual is denied any right,
privilege, or benefit that he would otherwise be entitled by Federal Law, or for which he would otherwise be eligible, as a result of the maintenance of
such material, such material shall be provided to
such individual, except to the extent that the disclosure of such material would reveal the identity
of a source who furnished information to the Government under an express promise that the identity
of the source would be held in confidence, or, prior
to the effective date of this section, under an implied promise that the identity of the source would
be held in confidence;

"(3) maintained in connection with providing protec-
tive services to the President of the United States or

other individuals pursuant to Section 3056 of title 18;

"(4)   required by statute to be maintained and used solely as statistical records;

"(5)   investigatory material compiled solely for the purpose of determining suitability, eligibility, or qualifications for Federal civilian employment, military service, Federal contracts, or access to classified information, but only to the extent that the disclosure of such material would reveal the identity of a source who furnished information to the Government under an express promise that the identity of the source would be held in confidence, or, prior to the effective date of this section, under an implied promise that the identity of the source would be held in confidence;

"(6)   testing or examination material used solely to determine individual qualifications for appointment or promotion in the Federal service the disclosure of which would compromise the objectivity or fairness of the testing or examination process; or

"(7)   evaluation material used to determine potential for promotion in the armed services, but only to the extent that the disclosure of such material would reveal the identity of a source who furnished information to the Government under an express promise that the identity of the source would be held in confidence, or, prior to the effective date of this section, under an implied promise that the identity of the source would be held in confidence.

At the time rules are adopted under this subsection, the agency shall include in the statement required under section 553(c) of this title, the reasons why the system of records is to be exempted from a provision of this section.

"(l) ARCHIVAL RECORDS.—

"(1) Each agency record which is accepted by the Administrator of General Services for storage, processing, and servicing in accordance with section 3103 of title 44 shall, for the purposes of this section, be considered to be maintained by the agency which deposited the record and shall be subject to the provisions of this section. The Administrator of General Services shall not disclose the record except to the agency which maintains the record, or under rules established by that agency which are not inconsistent with the provisions of this section.

"(2) Each agency record pertaining to an identifiable individual which was transferred to the National Archives of the United States as a record which has sufficient historical or other value to warrant its continued preservation by the United States Government, prior to the effective date of this section, shall, for the purposes of this section, be considered to be maintained by the National Archives and shall not be subject to the provisions of this section, except that a statement generally describing such records (modeled after the requirements relating to records subject to subsections (e)(4)(A) through (G) of this section) shall be published in the *Federal Register*.

"(3) Each agency record pertaining to an identifiable individual which is transferred to the National Archives of the United States as a record which has sufficient historical or other value to warrant its continued preservation by the United States Government, on or after the effective date of this section, shall, for the purposes of this section, be considered to be maintained by the National Archives and shall be exempt from the requirements of this section except subsections (e)(4)(A) through (G) and (e)(9) of this section.

"(m)   GOVERNMENT CONTRACTORS.—When an agency provides by a contract for the operation by or on behalf of the agency of a system of records to accomplish an agency function, the agency shall, consistent with its authority, cause the requirements of this section to be applied to such system. For purposes of subsection (i) of this section any such contractor and any employee of such contractor, if such contract is agreed to on or after the effective date of this section, shall be considered to be an employee of an agency.

"(n)   MAILING LISTS.—An individual's name and address may not be sold or rented by an agency unless such action is specifically authorized by law. This provision shall not be construed to require the withholding of names and addresses otherwise permitted to be made public.

"(o)   REPORT ON NEW SYSTEMS.—Each agency shall provide adequate advance notice to Congress and the Office of Management and Budget of any proposal to establish or alter any system of records in order to permit an evaluation of the probable or potential effect of such proposal on the privacy and other personal or property rights of individuals or the disclosure of information relating to such individuals, and its effect on the preservation of the constitutional principles of federalism and separation of powers.

"(p)   ANNUAL REPORT.—The President shall submit to the Speaker of the House and the President of the Senate, by June 30 of each calendar year, a consolidated report, separately listing for each Federal agency the number of records contained in any system of records which were exempted from the application of this section under the provisions of subsections (j) and (k) of this section during the preceding calendar year, and the reasons for the exemptions, and such other information as indicates efforts to administer fully this section.

"(q) EFFECT OF OTHER LAWS.—No agency shall rely on any exemption contained in section 552 of this title to withhold from an individual any record which is otherwise accessible to such individual under the provisions of this section."

Sec. 4.

The Chapter analysis of chapter 5 of title 5, United States Code, is amended by inserting:

"552a. Records about individuals."

immediately below:

"552. Public information; agency rules, opinions, orders, and proceedings."

[Section 5 of the Privacy Act established a Privacy Protection Study Commission for a period of two years. Its term has now expired. Among other things, the Commission was charged with the responsibility of assessing the effectiveness of privacy protections throughout the society. In July 1977, it issued a report entitled "Personal Privacy in an Information Society" which proposed a series of recommendations directed toward safeguarding personal privacy in both the public and private sector. This report can be obtained from the Superintendent of Documents, Government Printing Office, Washington, D.C. 20420 for a charge of $5.]

Sec. 6.

The Office of Management and Budget shall—

(1) develop guidelines and regulations for the use of agencies in implementing the provisions of section

552a of title 5, United States Code, as added by section 3 of this Act; and

(2) provide continuing assistance to and oversight of the implementation of the provisions of such section by agencies.

Sec. 7.

(a) —

(1) It shall be unlawful for any Federal, State or local government agency to deny to any individual any right, benefit, or privilege provided by law because of such individual's refusal to disclose his social security account number.

(2) The provisions of paragraph (1) of this subsection shall not apply with respect to—

(A) any disclosure which is required by Federal statute, or

(B) the disclosure of a social security number to any Federal, State, or local agency maintaining a system of records in existence and operating before January 1, 1975, if such disclosure was required under statute or regulation adopted prior to such date to verify the identity of an individual.

(b) Any Federal, State, or local government agency which requests an individual to disclose his social security number to any Federal, State, or local agency maintaining a system of records in existence and operating before January 1, 1975, if such disclosure was required under statute or regulation adopted prior to such date to verify the identity of an individual.

(b) Any Federal, State, or local government agency which requests an individual to disclose his social security account number shall inform that individual whether that disclosure is mandatory or voluntary, by what statutory or other authority such number is solicited, and what uses will be made of it.

Sec. 8.

The provisions of this Act shall be effective on and after the date of enactment, except that amendments made by section 3 and 4 shall become effective 270 days following the day on which this Act is enacted.

Sec. 9.

There is authorized to be appropriated to carry out the provisions of section 5 of this Act for fiscal years 1975, 1976, and 1977 the sum of $1,500,000, except that not more than $750,000 may be expended during any such fiscal year.

Approved December 31, 1974

APPENDIX C—ADDRESSES

ACTION:
  ACTION
  806 Connecticut Avenue, N.W.
  Washington, D.C. 20525
Administrative Conference of the United States:
  Administrative Conference of the United States
  Suite 500
  2120 L Street, N.W.
  Washington, D.C. 20037
Agriculture, Department of:
  Department of Agriculture
  Washington, D.C. 20250
Air Force, Department of the:
  Department of the Air Force
  The Pentagon
  Washington, D.C. 20330
Alcohol, Drug Abuse, and Mental Health Administration:
  Alcohol, Drug Abuse, and Mental Health Administration
  5600 Fishers Lane
  Rockville, Maryland 20857
Alcohol, Tobacco and Firearms, Bureau of:
  Bureau of Alcohol, Tobacco, and Firearms
  1200 Pennsylvania Avenue, N.W.
  Washington, D.C. 20226
American Battle Monuments Commission:
  American Battle Monuments Commission
  40014 Forrestal Bldg.
  Washington, D.C. 20314

Appalachian Regional Commission:
  Appalachian Regional Commission
  1666 Connecticut Avenue, N.W.
  Washington, D.C. 20235
Arms Control and Disarmament Agency:
  U.S. Arms Control and Disarmament Agency
  320 21st Street
  Washington, D.C. 20451
Army, Department of the:
  Department of the Army
  The Pentagon
  Washington, D.C. 20314
Census, Bureau of the:
  Bureau of the Census
  Federal Building 3
  Washington, D.C. 20233
Central Intelligence Agency:
  Central Intelligence Agency
  Washington, D.C. 20505
Civil Aeronautics Board:
  Civil Aeronautics Board
  1825 Connecticut Avenue, N.W.
  Washington, D.C. 20428
Civil Rights Commission:
  Civil Rights Commission
  1121 Vermont Avenue, N.W.
  Washington, D.C. 20425
Civil Service Commission:
  Civil Service Commission
  1900 E Street, N.W.
  Washington, D.C. 20415
Coastal Plains Regional Commission:
  Coastal Plains Regional Commission
  1725 K Street, N.W.
  Washington, D.C. 20006

Commerce, Department of:
Department of Commerce
Washington, D.C. 20230
Commodity Futures Trading Commission:
Commodity Futures Trading Commission
2033 K Street, N.W.
Washington, D.C. 20581
Community Services Administration:
Community Services Administration
1200 19th Street, N.W.
Washington, D.C. 20506
Comptroller of the Currency, Office of:
Office of Comptroller of the Currency
490 L'Enfant Plaza E., S.W.
Washington, D.C. 20219
Consumer Product Safety Commission:
Consumer Product Safety Commission
1111 18th Street, N.W.
Washington, D.C. 20207
Copyright Office:
Copyright Office
Library of Congress
Washington, D.C. 20559
Customs Service, United States:
U.S. Customs Service
1301 Constitution Avenue, N.W.
Washington, D.C. 20229
Defense, Department of:
Department of Defense
The Pentagon
Washington, D.C. 20301
Defense Contracts Audits Agency:
Defense Contracts Audits Agency
Cameron Station
Alexandria, Virginia 22314

Defense Intelligence Agency:
    Defense Intelligence Agency
    RDS-3A
    Washington, D.C. 20301
Defense Investigative Service:
    Defense Investigative Service
    D0020
    Washington, D.C. 20304
Defense Logistics Agency:
    Defense Logistics Agency
    Cameron Station
    Alexandria, Virginia 22314
Defense Mapping Agency:
    Defense Mapping Agency
    Naval Observatory
    Washington, D.C. 20305
Disease Control, Center for:
    Center for Disease Control
    Atlanta, Georgia 30333
Economic Development Administration:
    Economic Development Administration
    Department of Commerce
    14th & Constitution Avenue, N.W.
    Washington, D.C. 20230
Education, Office of:
    Office of Education
    400 Maryland Avenue, S.W.
    Washington, D.C. 20202
Energy, Department of:
    Department of Energy
    U.S. Department of Energy
    Washington, D.C. 20461
Environmental Protection Agency:
    Environmental Protection Agency
    401 M Street, S.W.
    Washington, D.C. 20460
Environmental Quality, Council on:

Council on Environmental Quality
722 Jackson Place, N.W.
Washington, D.C. 20006
Equal Employment Opportunity Commission:
Equal Employment Opportunity Commission
2401 E Street, N.W.
Washington, D.C. 20506
Export-Import Bank of the U.S.:
Export-Import Bank of the U.S.
811 Vermont Avenue, N.W.
Washington, D.C. 20571
Farm Credit Administration:
Farm Credit Administration
490 L'Enfant Plaza, S.W.
Washington, D.C. 20578
Federal Aviation Administration:
Federal Aviation Administration (FAA)
800 Independence Avenue, S.W.
Washington, D.C. 20591
Federal Bureau of Investigation:
Federal Bureau of Investigation
9th and Pennsylvania Avenue, N.W.
Washington, D.C. 20535
Federal Communications Commission:
Federal Communications Commission
1919 M Street, N.W.
Washington, D.C. 20554
Federal Deposit Insurance Corporation:
Federal Deposit Insurance Corporation
550 17th Street, N.W.
Washington, D.C. 20429
Federal Election Commission:
Federal Election Commission
1325 K Street, N.W.
Washington, D.C. 20463
Federal Highway Administration:

Federal Highway Administration
400 7th Street, S.W.
Washington, D.C. 20590
Federal Home Loan Bank Board:
Federal Home Loan Bank Board
320 First Street, N.W.
Washington, D.C. 20552
Federal Maritime Commission:
Federal Maritime Commission
1100 L Street, N.W.
Washington, D.C. 20573
Federal Mediation and Conciliation Service:
Federal Mediation and Conciliation Service
2100 K Street, N.W.
Washington, D.C. 20427
Federal Power Commission:
Federal Power Commission
825 North Capitol Street
Washington, D.C. 20426
Federal Trade Commission:
Federal Trade Commission
6th and Pennsylvania Avenue, N.W.
Washington, D.C. 20580
Food and Drug Administration:
Food and Drug Administration
5600 Fishers Lane
Rockville, Maryland 20857
Foreign Claims Settlement Commission:
Foreign Claims Settlement Commission
1111 20th Street, N.W.
Washington, D.C. 20579
General Accounting Office:
General Accounting Office
441 G. Street, N.W.
Washington, D.C. 20548
General Services Administration:
General Services Administration

18th and F Streets, N.W.
Washington, D.C. 20405
Health Care Financing Administration:
Health Care Financing Administration
330 C Street, S.W.
Washington, D.C. 20201
Health, Education, and Welfare, Department of:
U.S. Department of Health, Education, and Welfare
200 Independence Avenue, S.W.
Washington, D.C. 20201
Health Resources Administration:
Health Resources Administration
3700 East West Highway
Hyattsville, Maryland 20782
Health Services Administration:
Health Services Administration
5600 Fishers Lane
Rockville, Maryland 20857
Housing and Urban Development, Department of:
Department of Housing and Urban Development
Washington, D.C. 20410
Immigration and Naturalization Service:
Immigration and Naturalization Service
425 I Street, N.W.
Washington, D.C. 20536
Indian Claims Commission:
Indian Claims Commission
1730 K Street, N.W.
Washington, D.C. 20006
Information Agency, U.S. (USIA):
U.S. Information Agency
1750 Pennsylvania Avenue, N.W.
Washington, D.C. 20547
Interior, Department of:
Department of the Interior

18th and C Street, N.W.
Washington, D.C. 20240
Internal Revenue Service:
    Internal Revenue Service
    1111 Constitution Avenue, N.W.
    Washington, D.C. 20224
International Development, Agency for (AID):
    Agency for International Development
    21st and Virginia Avenue, N.W.
    Washington, D.C. 20532
International Trade Commission, U.S.:
    U.S. International Trade Commission
    701 E Street, N.W.
    Washington, D.C. 20436
Interstate Commerce Commission:
    Interstate Commerce Commission
    12th and Constitution Avenue, N.W.
    Washington, D.C. 20423
Justice, Department of:
    Department of Justice
    Washington, D.C. 20530
Labor, Department of:
    Department of Labor
    Washington, D.C. 20210
Law Enforcement Assistance Administration:
    Law Enforcement Assistance Administration
    633 Indiana Avenue, N.W.
    Washington, D.C. 20531
Maritime Administration:
    Maritime Administration
    Washington, D.C. 20230
National Aeronautics and Space Administration:
    National Aeronautics and Space Administration
    400 Maryland Avenue, S.W.
    Washington, D.C. 20546

National Archives and Records Service:
    National Archives and Records Service
    Washington, D.C. 20408
National Credit Union Administration:
    National Credit Union Administration
    2025 M Street, N.W.
    Washington, D.C. 20456
National Endowment for the Arts:
    National Endowment for the Arts
    806 15th Street, N.W.
    Washington, D.C. 20506
National Endowment for the Humanities:
    National Endowment for the Humanities
    806 15th Street, N.W.
    Washington, D.C. 20506
National Highway Traffic Safety Administration:
    National Highway Traffic Administration
    400 7th Street, S.W.
    Washington, D.C. 20590
National Institute of Education:
    National Institute of Education
    1200-19th Street, N.W.
    Washington, D.C. 20208
National Institutes of Health:
    National Institutes of Health
    9000 Rockville Pike
    Rockville, Maryland 20014
National Labor Relations Board:
    National Labor Relations Board
    1717 Pennsylvania Avenue, N.W.
    Washington, D.C. 20570
National Oceanic and Atmospheric Administration:
    National Oceanic and Atmospheric Administration
    6010 Executive Blvd.
    Rockville, Maryland 20852

National Railroad Passenger Corporation:
    National Railroad Passenger Corporation (AMTRAK):
    955 North L'Enfant Plaza, S.W.
    Washington, D.C. 20024
National Science Foundation:
    National Science Foundation
    1800 G Street, N.W.
    Washington, D.C. 20550
National Security Agency:
    National Security Agency
    Fort George Meade, Maryland 20755
National Security Council:
    National Security Council
    Old Executive Office Building
    Washington, D.C. 20506
National Transportation Safety Board:
    National Transportation Safety Board
    800 Independence Avenue, S.W.
    Washington, D.C. 20594
Navy, Department of the:
    Department of the Navy
    The Pentagon
    Washington, D.C. 20350
Nuclear Regulatory Commission:
    Nuclear Regulatory Commission
    Washington, D.C. 20555
Occupational Safety and Health Review Commission:
    Occupational Safety and Health Review Commission
    1825 K Street, N.W.
    Washington, D.C. 20006
Office of Management and Budget:
    Office of Management and Budget
    Old Executive Office Building
    Washington, D.C. 20503
Overseas Private Investment Corporation:
    Overseas Private Investment Corporation

1129 20th Street, N.W.
Washington, D.C. 20527
Postal Service, U.S.:
    U.S. Postal Service
    475 L'Enfant Plaza, S.W.
    Washington, D.C. 20260
Prisons, Bureau of:
    Bureau of Prisons
    320 First Street, N.W.
    Washington, D.C. 20534
Public Health Service:
    Public Health Service
    200 Independence Avenue, S.W.
    Washington, D.C. 20201
Railroad Retirement Board:
    Railroad Retirement Board
    844 N. Rush Street
    Chicago, Illinois 60611
Renegotiation Board:
    Renegotiation Board
    2000 M Street, N.W.
    Washington, D.C. 20446
Secret Service:
    U.S. Secret Service
    1800 G Street, N.W.
    Washington, D.C. 20223
Securities and Exchange Commission:
    Securities and Exchange Commission
    500 North Capitol Street
    Washington, D.C. 20549
Selective Service System:
    Selective Service System
    600 E Street, N.W.
    Washington, D.C. 20435
Small Business Administration:
    Small Business Administration

1441 L Street, N.W.
Washington, D.C. 20416
Social Security Administration:
Social Security Administration
6401 Security Blvd.
Baltimore, Maryland 21235
State, Department of:
Department of State
Washington, D.C. 20520
Tennessee Valley Authority (TVA):
Tennessee Valley Authority
400 Commerce Avenue
Knoxville, Tennessee 37902
Transportation, Department of:
Department of Transportation
400 7th Street, S.W.
Washington, D.C. 20590
Treasury, Department of:
Department of the Treasury
1500 Pennsylvania Avenue, N.W.
Washington, D.C. 20220
Urban Mass Transit Administration:
Urban Mass Transit Administration
400 7th Street, S.W.
Washington, D.C. 20590
Veterans Administration:
Veterans Administration
Vermont Avenue, N.W.
Washington, D.C. 20420

Index

137